AF484662

THE GHANA MINING MENACE

GALAMSEY

THE GHANA MINING MENACE

GALAMSEY

The emergence of the mining menace in Ghana known as Galamsey. The sad story of a canker that has ruined the rich natural resources of Ghana such as fertile lands, forest reserves, water bodies and the youth. The blessing and curse of the abundance of gold in Ghana.

Richard Antwi-Boasiako

THE GHANA MINING MENACE GALAMSEY

E-ISBN: (979-8-218-54334-1)

ISBN: (979-8-218-54333-4)

Library of Congress Control Number: 2024922948

Printed in the United States of America

Dedication

My loving wife

Dr. Hermina Antwi-Boasiako

And loving children

Richard Antwi-Boasiako

Leslie Antwi-Boasiako

Rachel Antwi-Boasiako

Acknowledgement

I give special thanks to my parents Samuel Kwame Antwi-Boasiako and Susana Owusua for their hard work in my upbringing and instilling in me the discipline that has made me so proud of my heritage.

I acknowledge my older siblings Vera Antwi-Boasiako, Nana Boadi, Charles Antwi-Boasiako, and Hannah Amofa-Apenteng (stool name Nana Afia Koa Kani) for being my pacesetters. I will continue to appreciate what I learned from them, especially the history lessons on our rich culture.

I thank my childhood playmates for all the numerous memories which enabled me to come up with this book. Even though some of them are no longer with us, their contributions to this book will forever be cherished.

Finally, I am most grateful to my various teachers, extended family, and friends who in their own special ways crossed my path at a point in time and shaped my life.

Table of Contents

Part 1.1 (1) – Notwithstanding any law to the contrary, no person shall engage in or undertake any small-scale gold mining operation unless there is an existence in respect of such mining operation a license granted by the Secretary for Lands and Natural Resources or by an officer authorized in that behalf by the Secretary.

Small--Scale Gold Mining Law, 1989 – PNDCL 218

Preface

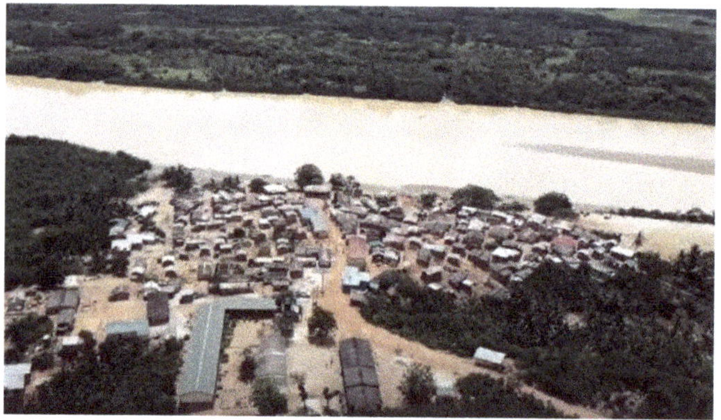

This book was written to highlight the adverse

impact of the illegal mining menace in Ghana called

Galamsey. I was born in a small village in Ghana on the

banks of the Birim river. I vividly recall the rich rural

experiences of life as a child in a village along a big

river. During my short stay at the village the Birim river

was fast-flowing and clean enough for one to see the

riverbed in shallow places. Walking to the riverbank

caused the fingerlings to swim into the deeper sections

of the river. As a child, one of the games was to run to

the riverbank to observe the small fishes or fingerlings

swim deeper. The source of life at the village was the

Birim river. I do not believe that is the case anymore.

My father's cocoa farm was along the river and my mother's staple crops farm was also along the river but on the opposite sides of the village. Farming was the main occupation in the village. Except Tuesdays and Sundays, most people spent the greater part of their day on the farm. Nearly all farmers had a lot of basket traps in the river all the time and checked them when they went to the farm. Crabs, lobsters and all kinds of fish were part of the daily diet. Even though I was a kid when I lived in the village I knew how to fish with the hook and line. The fish then were biting at anything used as bait. When I moved to the city and had to frequent the beach, my playmates were surprised I could swim very well. Living along a river makes one a natural swimmer. I was an adept swimmer at the age of seven even though I was never taught how to swim. I just played in the shallow areas of the river and with time I was able to float. You were considered a good swimmer in the village only when you were able to swim from one bank of the river to the other and then back. That was probably a distance of 100 feet.

This book will hopefully, document the drastic change in the rich experiences of life along rivers and forest areas in Ghana and what has become of that life in just a few years. My life in the village along the river was not always fun, especially when one had to toil daily on the farm. Looking back though, I wish I had more of that experience. When I was a kid, there was illegal mining even though we did not call it Galamsey. There were a few round holes along the footpaths to the farms. These holes were dug by the miners as they tried their luck. It was just a dent in the landscape in those days and involved a few locals using pickaxes and shovels to prospect for gold. They hardly dug six feet deep and wide enough to allow one to enter and throw away the dirt. This hardly posed any danger to humans. They were still dangerous to wildlife. The mining activities occurred only at night since it was illegal to mine in any form. From my memory, no one became rich from the illegal mining at the village, so it never attracted others, especially the youth to join. One was more likely to find the precious metals on the surface when it rained than digging the small round hole in the middle of the night. It was more profitable to have a good cocoa farm and a few foodstuff farms to produce your daily needs. My grandfather was able to cultivate enough cocoa farms to purchase two small buses.

When my father died, he was sent to the village where I was born to be buried. I spent one week at the land of my birth for the funeral. I had some free time after the ceremony to visit my favorite places in the village. When I visited the riverbank where we used to swim, it was covered with dirt. That means the kids do not go swimming anymore. The dirt was put there by the bulldozers of the miners (Galamsey). All along the sides of the river I observed pile after pile of yellowish mud. The river had increased in size due to the excavation along the banks. The color of the river was the most depressing part. The clear river I knew as a child had turned milky brown, not fit for even animals to drink. I was there for about half an hour and not a single fish jumped out of the river like they used to do. The fingerlings I grew to admire were no more. I was already feeling down because I had lost my father but the shock, I got from visiting the riverbank was worse. I had plans to visit my father's cocoa farm but was told one of my cousins sold it to the miners. It may seem very cruel but whether she wanted to sell it or not, she had no choice. The miners were already there with their bulldozers waiting to have the land sold to them or taking it upon themselves to dig at night. That is the sad part, you either sell to them or they dig at night when you are sound asleep at home. The destruction caused by mining along the Birim river is the same along most rivers in Ghana. I also visited my childhood city in the Western Region of Ghana. There are a few rivers on the way, the major one being the Pra river. The color of the Pra river was the same as that of the Birim river. It was not because the Birim river is a tributary of the Pra river, but the same fate has befallen the Pra. There is mining both along its banks and sadly in the middle of the river using a new technology called Changfa. The deadly Changfa machine floats on the river and mines the riverbed. The results are so devastating that one wonders how the menace was allowed to begin in the first place. The only water body that looked natural was the sea. I know that also has its own problem with sand winning. Some of the beaches in the country are depleted of sand due to illegal sand winning. The color of the sea along the coast of Ghana though is still blue.

The rivers are a small part of the mining destruction. Most of the devastation occurs deep in the forests. Ghana was blessed with a lot of forests and some of them were reserved. For some unknown reasons these miners believe the forest areas have more gold and have entered them to create large craters which are more dangerous than river mining. They have used excavators to remove the middle part of most of the rich forests in Ghana. Forest reserves are supposed to be out of bounds to everyone so one wonders how these miners were able to place excavators in them to cut down all the trees and reduce them to moonscape surfaces.

I intentionally omitted names of places and people in this book for obvious reasons. I hope this book will contribute toward bringing awareness of the harm caused by illegal small-scale mining. The paradox of this menace is that everyone is blaming others for causing it. When you listen to very intelligent people discussing the solution to stopping this menace, it quickly turns into political accusations and the blame game turns to insults. The last time I sojourned in my village, I could not fathom how a fast-flowing river had turned into a slow-moving enlarged river such as one will expect when a river is about to enter the sea. The damage done unfortunately may be irreversible. It may take generations to restore them. I hope and pray I will see a return to normality in my lifetime. It is all in the hands of the people and the government. The citizens must give up the habit.

Part 1.1 (2) – An application for a license under this section shall be made in such forms as the Secretary may direct to the relevant District Centre of the designated area and shall be accompanied by such fee as the Secretary may prescribe.

Small--Scale Gold Mining Law, 1989 – PNDCL 218

Chapter 1
The Mining Laws

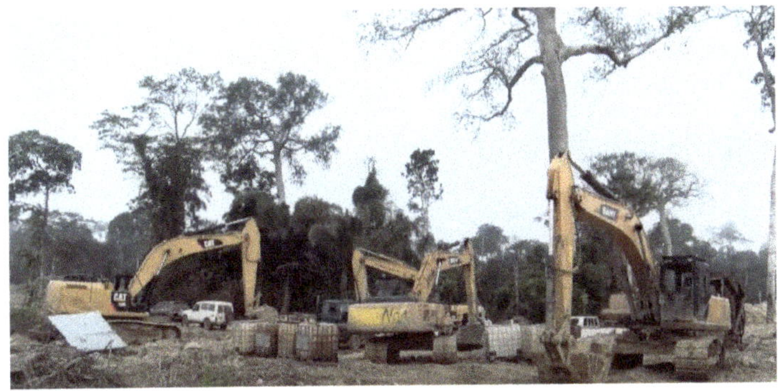

Destroyed Forest

Ghana is endowed with vast mineral resources. Before the country got independence from the British it was called the Gold Coast. Gold has always been abundant, and it is manifested in the way the chiefs display it during gatherings. Gold is also what led to the war between the British and the Asantes in the "Golden Stool War" or "Yaa Asantewaa War". Mining for these precious metals has been ongoing since the land was inhabited by humans. Initially it was done primitively by a few people digging holes that did not disturb the natural environment. There is also commercial mining done by multinationals in areas agreed upon between the mining companies and the government. After large scale mining in a designated area is over, scavengers enter the mining pits gathering whatever they could find to sell. It was this way of gathering and selling these leftover rare precious metals from abandoned mines that gave birth to the name GALAMSEY (Gather and Sell). It was not a bad name initially until the mining menace started. The name Galamsey is now generally used to refer to illegal small-scale mining, that is mining without a license.

Small scale mining activities were done illegally, mostly at night. The irresponsible way of mining and the havoc it was causing forced the government of Ghana to come up with the idea of granting mining licenses to streamline it. In 1989 the government of Ghana enacted the Small-Scale Mining Act (PNDCL 218) which was later in 2006 integrated into the Mining Act 703. The government also repealed the 1932 Mercury Ordinance and promulgated the Mercury Law (PNDCL 217), making it legal for small scale miners to obtain mercury from authorized dealers. Just like most laws in the country, these were great laws, with a lot of problems when it comes to enforcing them. These laws have not been able to eradicate the mining destruction that led to their enactment. The following are a few of the remarkable sections in PNDCL 218.

Part 1.2 - No license for small-scale gold mining operations shall be granted to

a) any person who is not a citizen of Ghana

b) any person who has not attained the age of eighteen years

c) any person who is not registered by the district center in the designated area.

Part 1.8 -

a) the district center shall compile a register of all small-scale miners

b) supervise and monitor the operations

c) advise and provide training facilities

d) submit to the Minerals Commission reports on small-scale mining activities within the district.

Part 11- (Operations of small-scale gold miners).

Part 11.11 - A person licensed to mine gold under this Law may win, mine and produce gold by any effective and efficient method and shall in his operations observe good mining practices, health and safety rules and pay due regard to the protection of the environment.

Part 11.12 - Where a license is granted in a designated area to any person other than the owner of the land, the licensee shall pay to the owner of the land such compensation for the use of the land as the Secretary may in consultation with the Minerals Commission and the Land Valuation Board determine.

Part 11.13 - No small-scale gold miner shall use any explosives in his operations.

Part 11.14 - A small-scale gold miner may purchase from any authorized mercury dealer such quantities of mercury as may be reasonably necessary for the purpose of his mining operations.

Every mineral in its natural state in, under and upon the land, rivers, streams watercourses throughout the country is vested in the President of Ghana in trust of the people. The issuance of mining license is the sole prerogative of the Secretary of Lands and Natural

Resources (Minerals Commission of Ghana). The chiefs who are most of the time the owners of the land are not involved in issuing the license. This creates a rift between the chiefs, the people and the miners. The valuation of the land does not include any input from the landowner. The willingness of the farmer to sell the land is also not considered. Most cocoa farms are passed from generation to generation sustaining the family. It becomes a major dilemma when a stranger shows up with a piece of paper stating he has been granted a license to do small-scale mining in the area. Miners do not reclaim the land after their operations, meaning the land is destroyed after their mining operations.

Most people would rather look for these precious metals themselves these days on their farms than allow someone with a license to come for them. These laws put too much faith in the gold miner. A miner in the middle of nowhere will prefer blasting any boulders to using a chisel and harmer which is too labor intensive and slow. A typical small-scale gold miner cannot be asked to observe good mining practices, health and safety rules, and pay due regard to the protection of the environment. Most miners are not knowledgeable in mining hazards and do not read the mining laws. Their main objective is to maximize profits.

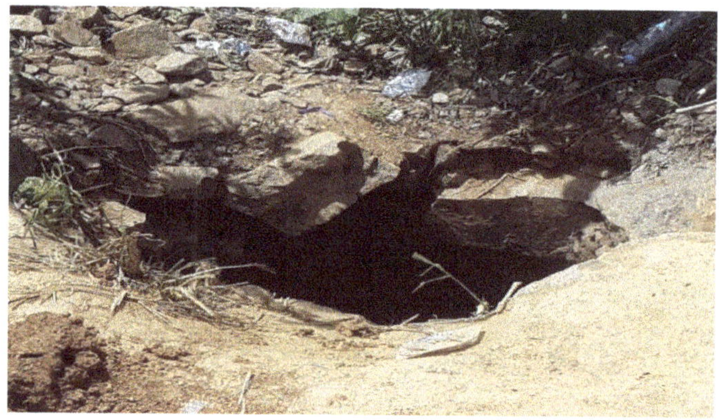

Dangerous Gold Pit

Legal small-scale mining is very expensive. The average small-scale miner cannot afford the cost involved in getting a license, compensating the owner of the land and renting equipment for the operations. Most of these miners therefore front for foreigners who have the capital. This makes it difficult to enforce section 2 of the law regarding foreigners. The mercury law is a short document, but these two areas are challenging.

Section 4 –

1. Notwithstanding anything contained in any enactment to the contrary licensed small-scale gold miners may

purchase from licensed mercury dealers such reasonable quantities of mercury as may be shown to be necessary for the purpose of their mining operations.

2. Small-scale gold miners shall observe good mining practices in the use of mercury for carrying out mining operations,

The use of mercury is one of the most devastating parts during small-scale mining, especially those mining very close to water bodies and inside the rivers. Mercury bonds to the gold in small-scale mining operations to form an amalgam but it is extremely harmful to the human nervous system. The mercury unfortunately gets into the water bodies and eventually to the people either from drinking the water or eating the fish. These mining and mercury laws are basically expecting the miners to be good citizens. The law asks the miners to observe good mining practices. Every miner will therefore perform their operations the way they see fit. Inspectors will also find it difficult to distinguish the good mining practice from the bad ones. The lack of specific quantities for the mercury purchase is a recipe for failure. If a miner is asked to buy the quantity of mercury as may be necessary for their operations, then any quantity is going to be necessary. The limit will depend on how much the miner can afford. It will remove any ambiguity if the quantity of mercury any miner can purchase is based for instance on the size of their concessions. Leftover mercury is never returned.

Since legal small-scale mining is very expensive, most small-scale miners are illegal miners. Even if all the bottlenecks in obtaining a mining license are solved or removed, doing illegal small-scale mining will still be more profitable to the average miner. The illegal small-scale miner will not pay the landowner, will not have to travel to the capital to chase a license and will not be subjected to any inspections. This is a very dangerous trend in the country. Many of these miners do not observe safe mining practices under the mandate in the mining license. The average miner is not educated enough to know most of the adverse effects of mercury. They also do not know the hazards of inhaling the toxic chemicals in the atmosphere around the mining sites. They continue to ply their trade till they become too weak to work.

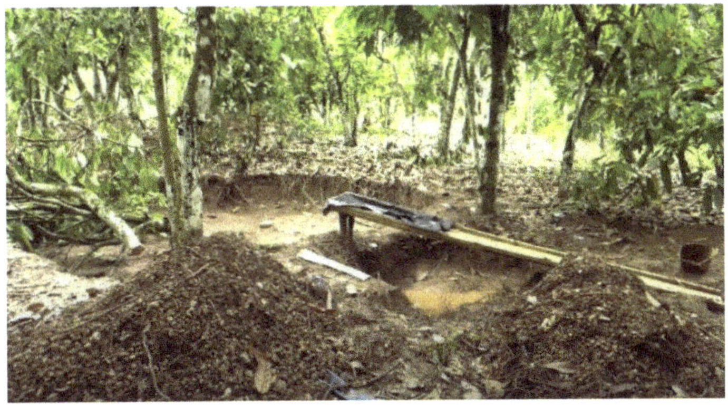

Mining in a Cocoa Farm

The most adversely affected sector is the cocoa industry. Ghana used to be the number one producer of cocoa in the world. These farms used to provide the family with all the cash they needed for the year. With the advent of illegal mining, the income from cocoa has lost its value. Most farmers now prospect on their own farms or sell the farm to the miners to get what the farm will generate in a decade. The mess is going to affect the next generation the hardest. There will be no more Abusua (family) cocoa farms to inherit. The land for growing food stuff is now made up of craters and cannot be farmed. In effect the cash provider is gone and there is nowhere to grow the basic staple needs. This is what the Ghana greed has created in a developing country.

The granting of mining license is done in the capital of the country, Accra. The legal miner with a license moves to the site whether it is the correct location or not. Since there is no strict verification and supervision done by the issuing authority, it becomes difficult to know if the miner is at the licensed location. Most of these miners are therefore able to use the same license to mine multiple locations. In most developing countries those who obtain the license are not the actual miners. Some of these license owners do not even know the location of their concession. They obtain the license and sell it to the actual miners.

The mining license is for legal small-scale mining. There is no law regulating the illegal small-scale mining but most miners in Ghana fall under the illegal small-scale miners' group. This creates a great challenge to the country. With the lack of any meaningful youth employment in the county, illegal mining has provided for most of the families in the rural areas. The negative effects of improper mining methods far outweigh any benefit the miners are getting. This poses a great danger to the people of the whole country, and future generations. The idea of granting a mining license to local miners can be described as a failed policy.

Community mining license is a good policy allowing the local community to benefit from the reserves in their local community. The only problem is that there are not many experts to monitor and control their activities. Ghana has abundance of experts who can help control irresponsible mining. Unfortunately, these experts are either not engaged or live in the capital city and monitor from the luxury of their offices. When they manage to go near the mining sites, they want to get there in their luxury four-wheel drive vehicles. This has and will always be a challenge in dealing with a situation that requires constant vigilant supervision and control.

The Minerals Commission is often blamed for allowing this evil to go on because they do not arrest the perpetrators. Expecting any government agency to go and arrest illegal miners is pushing them in harm's way. No one will dare go near well-protected armed mining operations except the national security agencies.

Part 11.11 - A person licensed to mine gold under this Law may win, mine and produce gold by any effective and efficient method and shall in his operations observe good mining practices, health and safety rules and pay due regard to the protection of the environment.

Small--Scale Gold Mining Law, 1989 – PNDCL 218

Chapter 2

Types of Galamsey

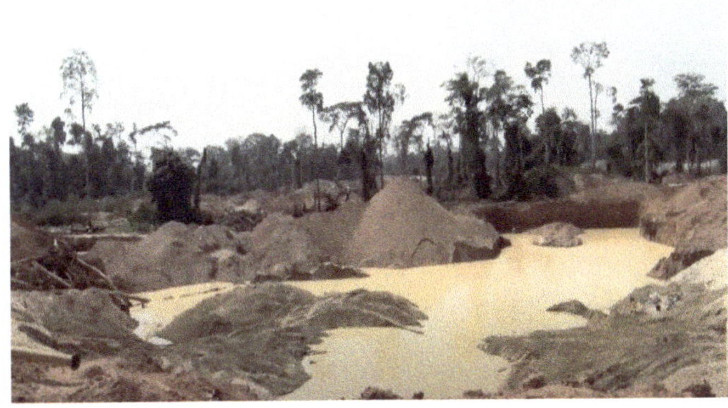

There are numerous ways to get gold from the ground. The method used by a miner depends on many factors, such as the nature and quantity of the deposits, the tools available to the miner, and the risk the miner is willing to take. Each of these methods has its own risks and affects the natural environment negatively. These are a few of the methods regularly used in gold mining in Ghana.

The Underground Pit (Stoping) – This method is one of the oldest mining methods and encompasses the mining of the gold bearing rocks from the underground pit. It may be the most dangerous of all the mining methods. This type is also labor intensive. The process involves digging or excavating large underground rooms or stops. When the surrounding rocks are not strong enough to permit blasting and drilling, they are supported artificially by wooden structures. The entrance is usually narrow to allow one to enter and the excavation is done in various directions.

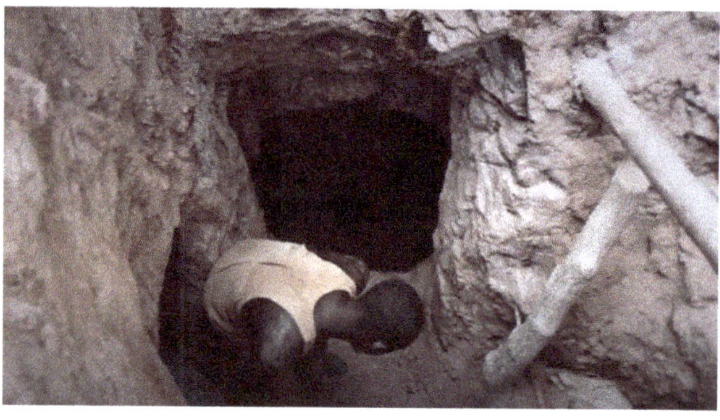

The main risk associated with underground pits is the frequent collapse of the supporting structures. Most of these miners do not have any engineering background. They just assume the structure they erect will be able to support the surrounding rocks, but most casualties are caused by the collapsed pit. Another issue which these miners have little knowledge of is aeration or ventilation. Every underground pit needs a method of clearing hazardous gases and dust created by constant blasting and drilling activities. Proper ventilation is therefore essential to control the underground air quality and temperature. Both the underground rocks and the human body generate heat. If the underground pit is not properly ventilated, gas explosions occur. There is also extreme temperature and poor air quality leading to long-term health problems.

The Dig and wash – This method is one of the most popular methods and perhaps less risky. It also involves very basic tools such as pickaxes, spades, shovels and a washing tool. It needs water to wash, making this type of mining occurring near water bodies. The process is basically digging the materials containing the alluvial gold deposits and then washing them using very simple tools.

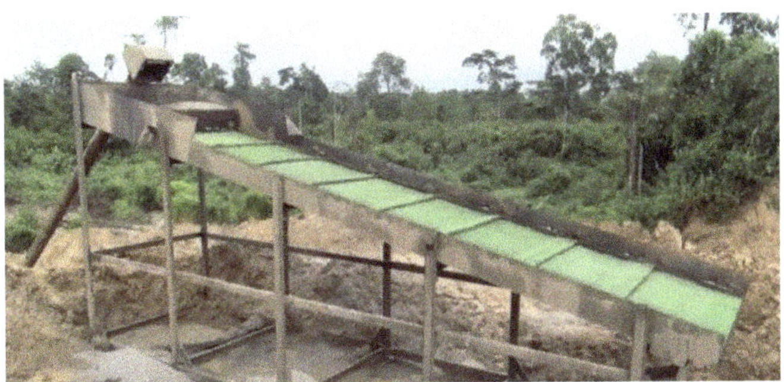

Washing Tray

Depending on the finances of the miners some can afford to rent or buy generators to pump the water onto the washing trays. Washing is mostly done on the banks of rivers, but a few miners do the washing standing in the river. Eventually, all the toxic water from washing by the miners ends up in the rivers.

The Chisel and hammer – This method is very manual and not popular. The vegetation and topsoil are removed leaving the hard rock formations. A chisel and hammer are used to break up the rocks. The big pieces of rock are then sent to a crusher to be crushed into fines. The gold particles are recovered from the fine materials. The miners prefer using explosives to blast the rocks to chisel and hammer as it takes less time and manpower.

Alluvial mining – This method occurs near water bodies and is used to mine mineral deposits in streams and other water bodies. Alluvial deposits are formed when the mineral is eroded from their source and deposited in a new location by the water body. The minerals normally deposit according to their weight. Miners use simple tools such as shovels to dig and sift through the soft mud of the riverbed.

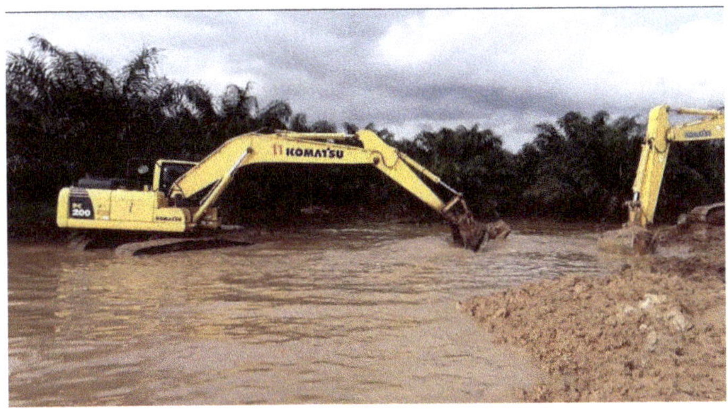

Mining in the middle of a river

This type of mining is not very profitable but has a high impact on the environment. It disturbs the flow of the river especially when the miners divert the natural course of the river. The recent introduction of excavators has made this type of mining a national pandemic as drinking water is being wasted for a fistful of gold. The use of mercury also pollutes the water body killing the living things in the river. Most illegal miners are now able to rent generators to pump out the water. The diesel used by these generators also ends up in the water body which is eventually passed on to the citizens of Ghana both in the rural areas and the cities.

Surface Mining – This method is very destructive as it clears a large area of land for a handful of gold. This is practiced in land-locked areas. With the use of a bulldozer a vast area of the vegetation is cleared and excavated searching for gold. Since the operation is mostly in the middle of the forest areas it is often very difficult for the authorities to notice their activities until they are done with the operations.

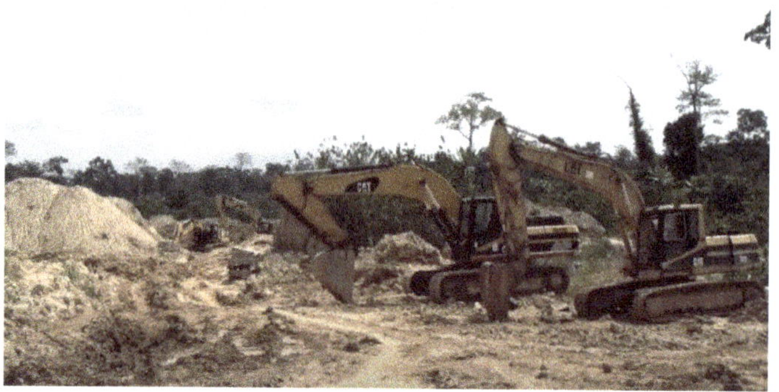

Surface Mining Site

The miners build their camp and live as a community in the forest. They dig wells for the water they need. After one area is depleted of resources, they move camp to a new area leaving behind a moonscape surface. An area is abandoned when the returns are far below the expenses. The land is usually not reclaimed, making it a wasteland unsuitable for farming.

The Changfa – This technique is quite recent and involves the use of the diesel powered Changfa machine to extract the Gold. The machine can simultaneously mine and extract the gold. It can be used in both land-locked areas and on water bodies. It requires water for its operations. Miners therefore prefer to operate it near or on water bodies.

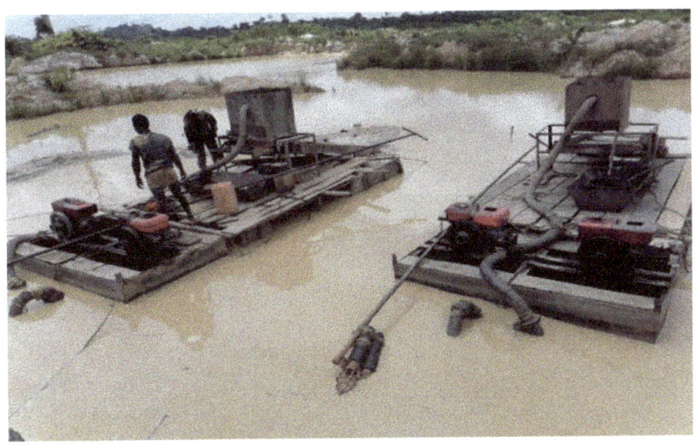

Changfa machines on a river

The machine has two pipes. One shoots water with high pressure on the bottom layer of the riverbed. The other pipe sucks in the dispersed mud onto a ramp. As the mud water flows down the ramp, a mat sieves out the heavier particles including the gold. The use of Changfa machine is perhaps the most devastating type of illegal mining. Even though it can be used in land-locked areas it is more profitable to use it right in the middle of the river. It is also difficult for the authorities to arrest them since the navy is the only government agency well equipped to deal with swift swimmers. All the activities are done on the river, meaning when the mercury is applied the waste is poured into the river.

The Abandoned Underground Shaft – This method is one of the oldest forms of illegal mining. The main concentration area is the Tarkwa Nsuaem District with the big mining companies namely Gold Fields Ghana Limited, Gold Star Bogoso-Prestea Mines, AngloGold Iduapriem and Nsuta Manganese and Gold Mines.

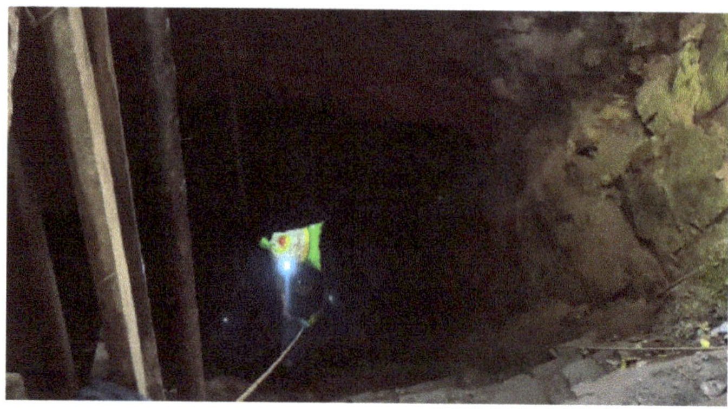

Abandoned Underground Shaft

This type requires having a Millhouse nearby to process the gold. It involves the blasting, dewatering and hauling of the ore from these abandoned shafts to the nearby Millhouse. Some miners now encroach on the active mines of the multinational mining companies.

Part 11.14 - A small-scale gold miner may purchase from any authorized mercury dealer such quantities of mercury as may be reasonably necessary for the purpose of his mining operations.

Small--Scale Gold Mining Law, 1989 – PNDCL 218

Chapter 3

Effects of Galamsey on the rivers

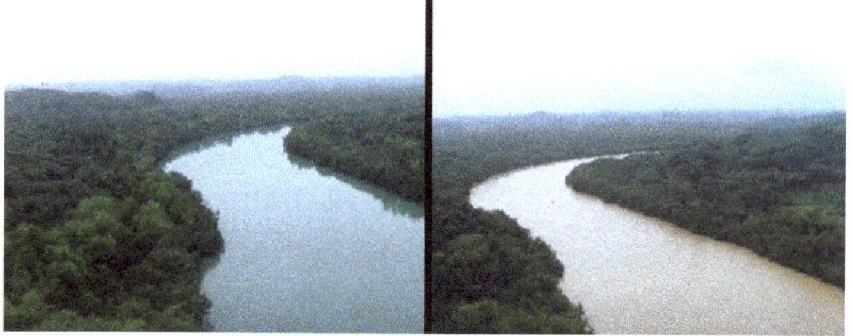

Before and after of river Ankobra

Ghana is a developing country. It is less industrialized and more agricultural. That means the country is highly dependent on the land and rivers to survive. The main occupations are farming and fishing. Cocoa is the main foreign exchange earner and most of the citizens are in one way or the other connected to it. Cocoa is not directly consumed in the country, so all the farmers have other farms that produce their daily needs. They also get their fish from the rivers. Apart from the few cities which are lucky to have pipe borne water, the rivers provide the main source of water. To get the pipe borne water a river is dammed and treated. It is therefore unthinkable to imagine anyone destroying the rivers in Ghana.

No single mining type is more destructive of rivers than the other. All the illegal mining activities are destructive of the water bodies. Dredging and washing near and inside the water bodies have all altered the ecosystems of Ghana. One way to know the harm done to the water bodies is to measure their turbidity levels. Turbidity is the concentration of materials suspended in a water sample and how it affects light penetration. This simply means the relative clarity of water. One does not need to measure this to know that all the rivers in Ghana are in jeopardy. The World Health Organization (WHO) says that the maximum amount of turbidity that should be present in water is 5 Nephelometric Turbidity Units (NTU). There are two main standard units for measuring water turbidity. The other is Formazin Nephelometric Units FNU). Depending on the system used in your country you may see NTU or FNU. In all cases the higher the number the more the water is polluted.

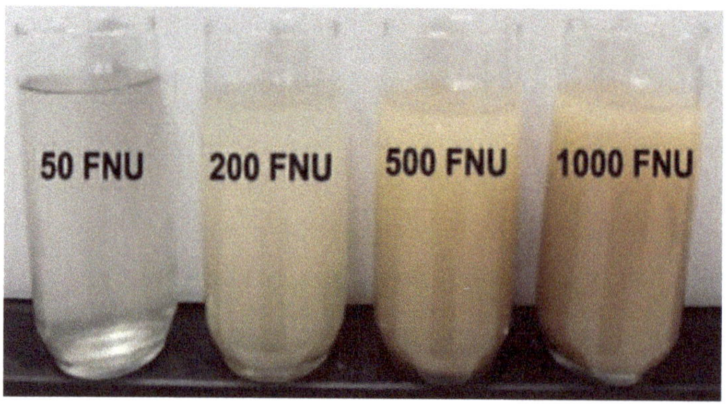

Water Turbidity

The main sources of fish are from sea fishing and river fishing. The sea fishing is mainly done by people along the coast of Ghana. Other fishermen ply their trade in the numerous rivers in the country. With the current turbidity of rivers in Ghana, it will be a miracle for fish to survive in the rivers. Apart from the color being milky brown the rivers are also filled with mercury and cyanide. The illegal mining has destroyed the livelihood of local river fishermen. The farmers who relied on placing their basket traps for their daily fish needs are also doomed.

The residents in the bigger towns and cities are not spared this menace. The main source of their water needs used to be from the pipe borne water at home. Unfortunately, they now use pipe borne water for other things excluding dinking. They need to buy bottled water or sachet water to drink and cook. The intake of the treatment plants cannot cope with the high turbidity of the rivers. The illegal mining on rivers has directly and indirectly impacted water treatment plants in the country. Some turbidity levels have reached 14,000 NTU. Treatment machines that are supposed to last 30 years now last 10 years due to the waste in the water. It costs the water companies much more now to buy the chemicals to treat the water. The machines are also stopped frequently to clean them. When the silt gets to a certain level the plant is completely shut down. The rising cost of treating water is making the Ghana Water Company financially unviable.

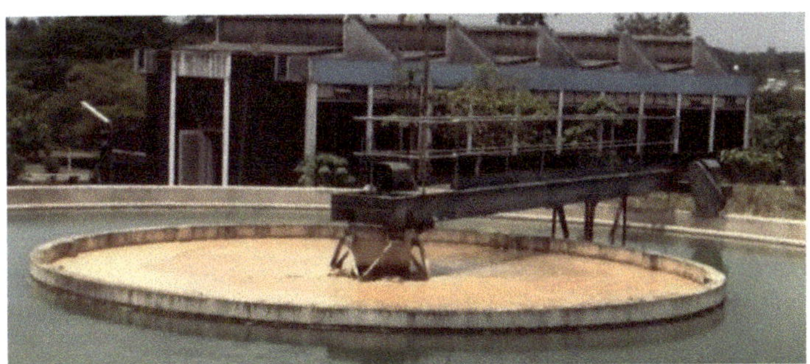

Water Treatment Eastern Region

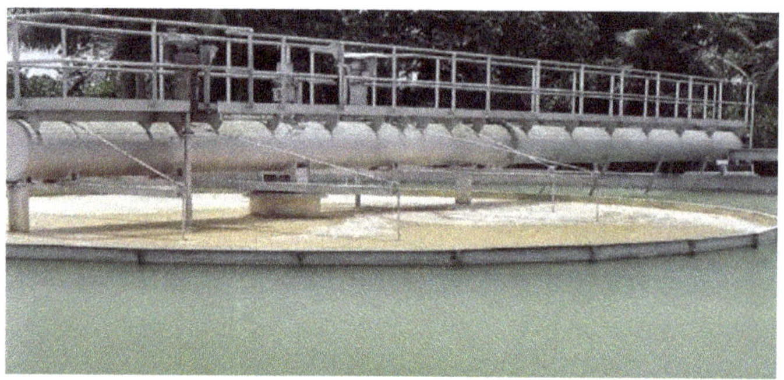

Water Treatment Central Region

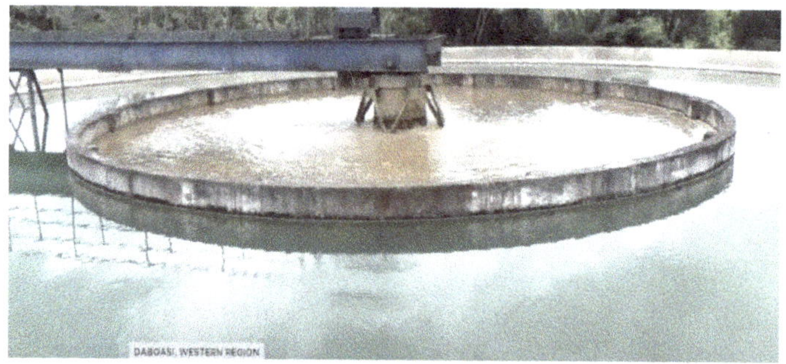

Water Treatment Western Region

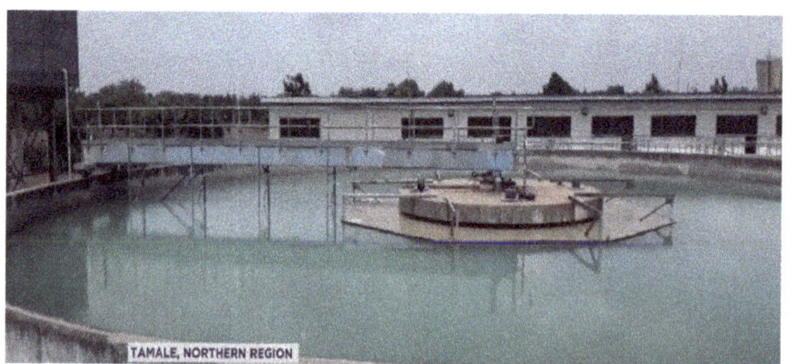

Water Treatment Northern Region

The rich can buy bottled water, but others buy the locally made sachet water. The wildlife on the other hand has no option but to drink the murky water. Hopefully, they get pools of water from the rainfall. There is no way they can drink what we see in the rivers and survive. Most villages and towns in Ghana are located near sources of water. A single river therefore serves all the towns and villages scattered on its banks. Any mining activity at any part of the river deprives all the downstream inhabitants of their livelihood.

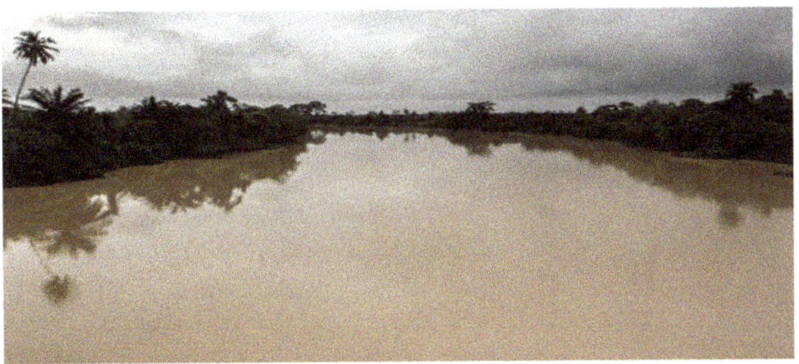

River Pra

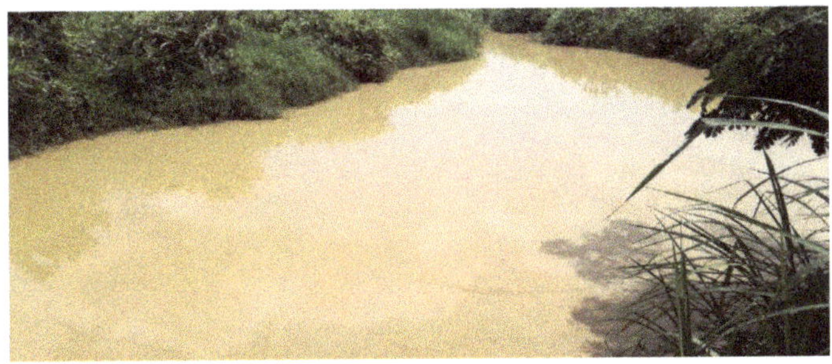

River Birim

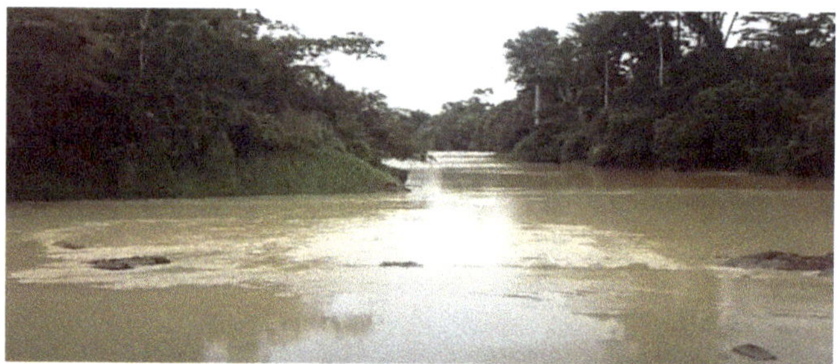

River Offin

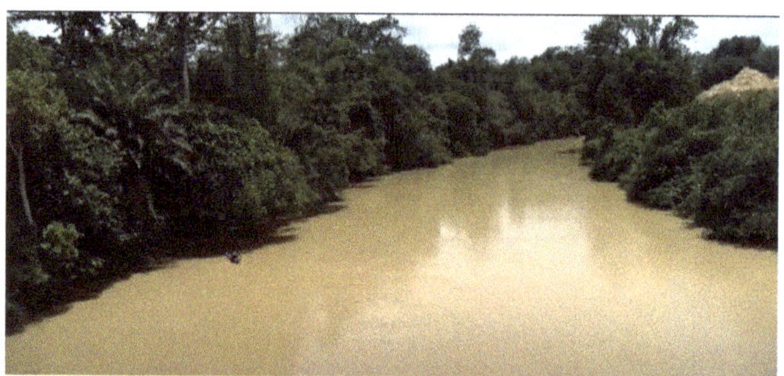

River Tano

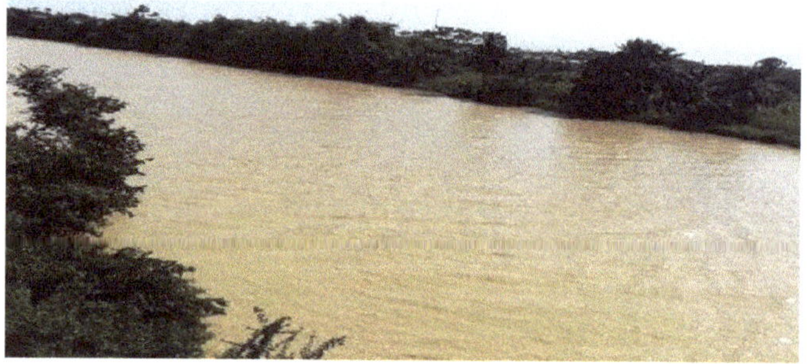

River Oda

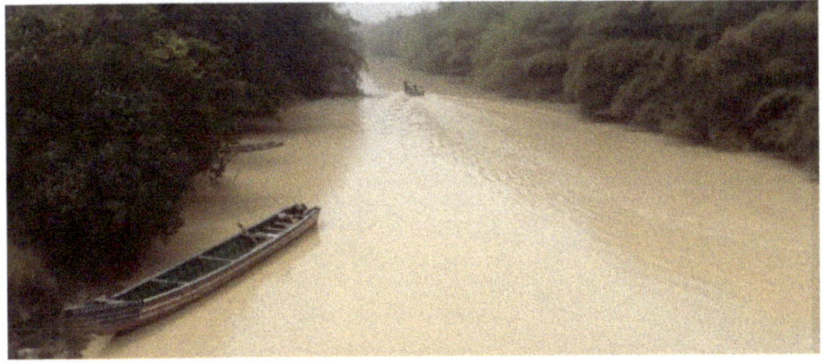

River Ankobra

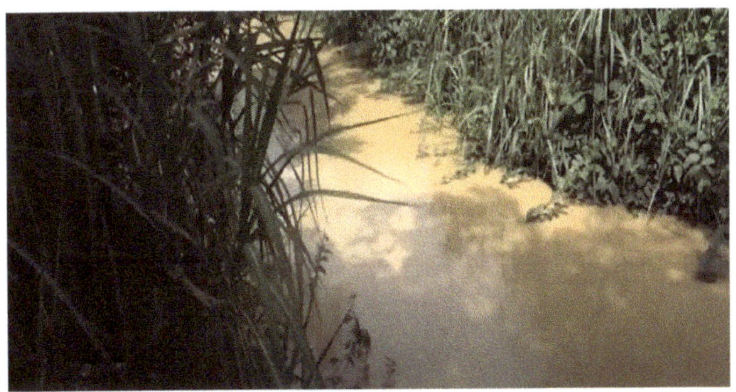

River Densu

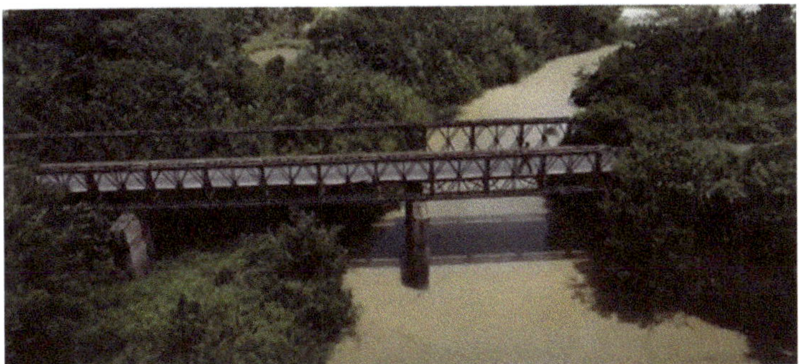

River Anuru

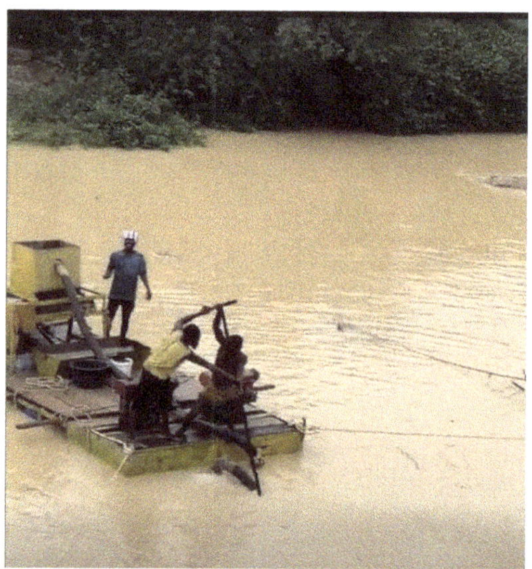

River Bonsa

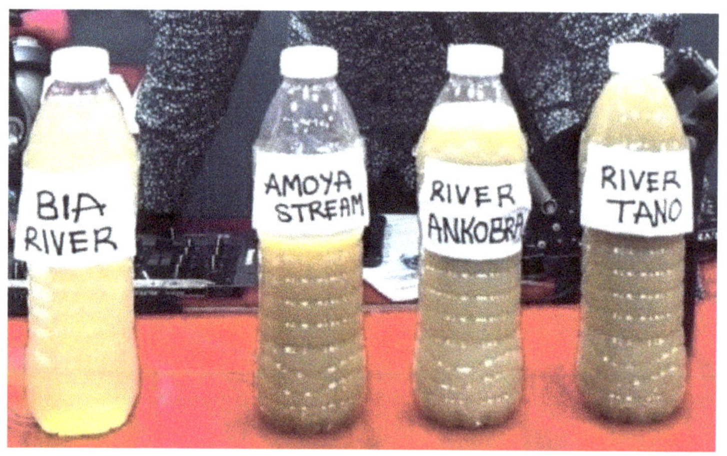

The main source of drinking water in the country now is Sachet water. According to the 2021 Population and Housing Census (PHC), the percentage using Sachet water was 37.4 per cent while pipe-borne water was 31.7 per cent. That means, a great portion of the population depends on these rivers and streams being destroyed by greed. The treatment plants are spending a lot more to treat the water and still sending undrinkable water to their customers.

According to the Water Resources Commission in Ghana, the turbidity levels of rivers in the country are between 504 NTU and 3,880 NTU. This far exceeds the acceptable numbers of 5 NTU for drinking and 80 NTU to 150 NTU for cooking. Water is life and most countries do everything in their power to protect what they have. Countries even go to war to protect water rights. Ghana has an abundant supply of water, but the greed of the current generation is turning the country into a water deficient state. It is not easy treating water filled with mercury and cyanide. More chemicals are applied to get rid of them, but every chemical is unsafe for human consumption.

Section 17 of the Ghana Mining and Minerals Act is one of the most unforeseen damages caused by the Act. It has led to river courses being altered and destroyed by a few greedy individuals to the detriment of the whole country.

Section 17 - Water right

Subject to obtaining the requisite approvals or licenses under the Water Resources Commission Act 1996 (Act 522), a holder of a mineral right may, for purposes of or ancillary to the mineral operations, obtain, divert, impound, convey and use water from a river, stream, underground reservoir or watercourse within the land the subject of the mineral act.

MINERALS AND MINING ACT, 2006 (ACT 703)

Water bodies in the country will only be safe from miners when this unconscionable law is repealed.

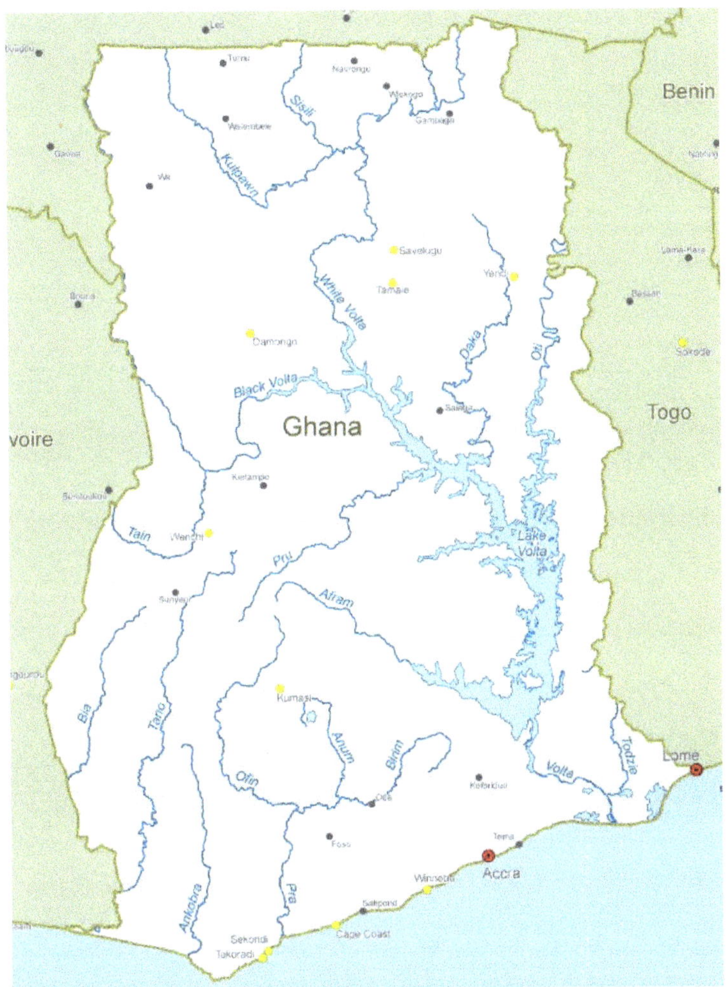

Ghana Rivers map

Part 11.12 - Where a license is granted in a designated area to any person other than the owner of the land, the licensee shall pay to the owner of the land such compensation for the use of the land as the Secretary may in consultation with the Minerals Commission and the Lands Valuation Board determine.

Small--Scale Gold Mining Law, 1989 – PNDCL 218

Chapter 4

Effects of Galamsey on the Land

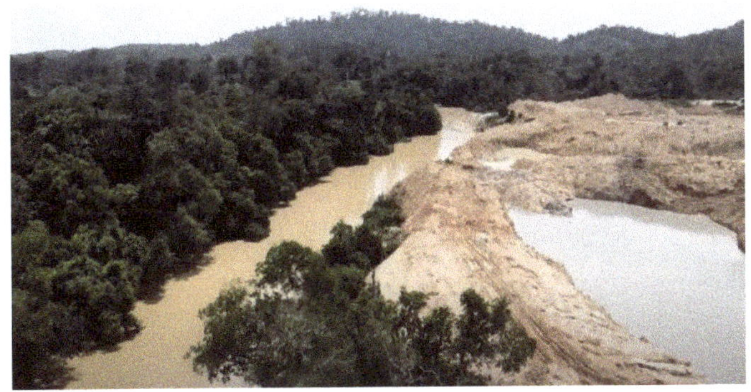

Destroyed Land

Ghana is blessed with a lush vegetation. There is the coastal and northern savanna and a middle 30,000 square miles forest zone. With two main rainy seasons the middle belt is always green. The land is also rich in animal life. Parts of the forest are reserved to protect and conserve the ecosystem. Ghana has two types of these forests namely the production forest reserves and protected forest reserves. The main reserved forests are:

Achimota Forest Reserve

Ankasa Conservation Area

Assin Attandanso Game Production Reserve

Asubima Forest Reserve

Atewa Range Forest Reserve

Ayum Forest Reserve

Boin Tano Forest Reserve

Bonsam Bepo Forest Reserve

Draw River Forest Reserve

Gbele Game Production Reserve

Kalakpa Game Production Reserve

Krokosua Hills Forest Reserve

Mamiri Forest Reserve

Tano Nimiri Forest Reserve

Apart from those government reserved forests there are some forests reserved by traditional rulers for the burial of chiefs called *"Nsaman Po"* (Forest of the spirits). Since these forests are out of bounds wildlife has always been in abundance. Hunters who get closer to them can hunt some of the animals that stray from these reserved forests. The forests also protect the rivers as most of the rivers have their source in the middle of the forest.

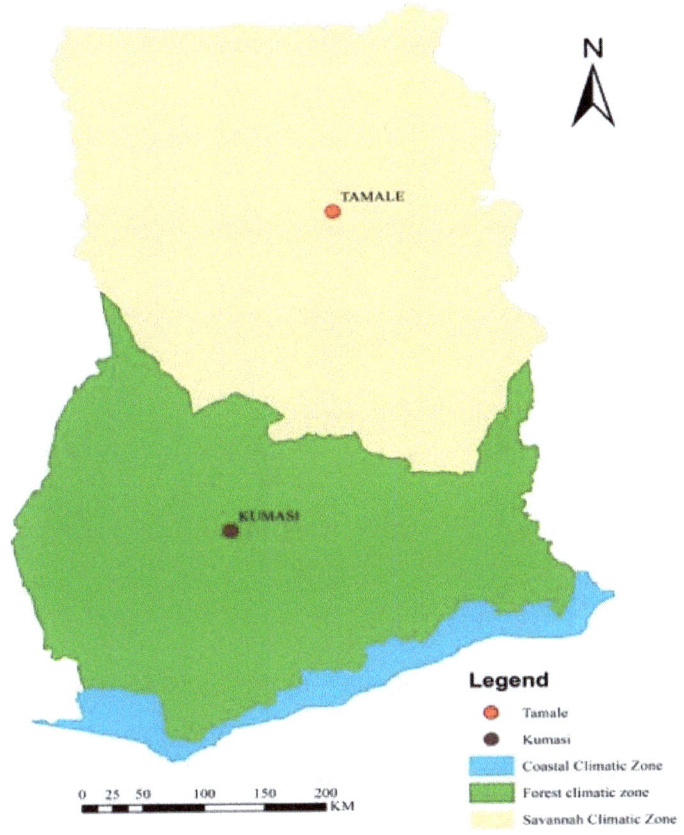

These forests were well protected until the Ghanaian greed started. The average Ghanaian is afraid of the dark especially being in the forest at night. Those forests reserved by our ancestors for burial of chiefs were never entered by the average Ghanaian. With the advent of illegal gold mining all these fears are now a thing of the past. Gold miners now prefer to ply their trade in the virgin forests at night. They manage to get into the middle part of the forest to prospect for gold. These forests look natural and undisturbed from afar. The devastation becomes noticeable only when one gets closer to the middle part.

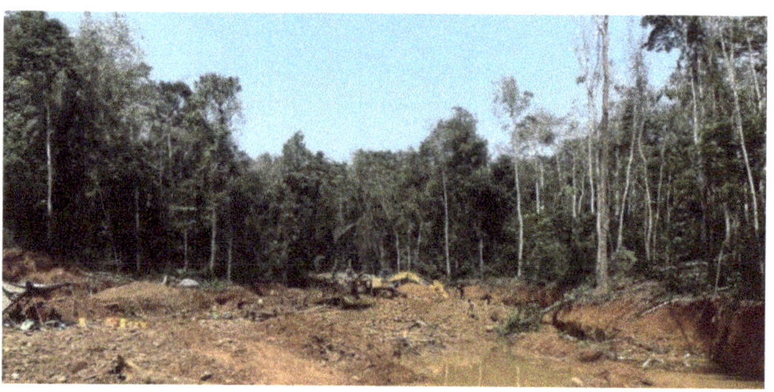

Atewa Forest

Around fifty two percent of the labor force in Ghana is engaged in agriculture. The 2017/2018 Ghana Census of Agriculture report stated that over 11.3 million Ghanaians engaged in Agriculture. Ghana's primary farming system is known as the bush fallow system. This is the system where a plot of land is allowed to rest for a period of one to three years to recoup its fertility. Most farming lands now require a permanent fallow period due to mining. The main cash crops are cocoa, oil palm, coffee, cotton, tobacco and rubber. Maize, plantain, sorghum, millet, rice, groundnuts, cocoyam and cassava are the main staple food crops. The cash crops are usually mono cropped, with the staple crops being mixed cropped.

Most Ghanaian farmers in the forest areas rely on their cocoa farms for their annual family income and the various other farms for their staple food needs. For decades these cocoa farms sustained the whole family. This way of life came crushing down when the gold rush started. These farmers lived from one cocoa season to the next and received a lump sum once a year. Savings were not something most farmers could afford. The price of cocoa in 2021/2022 was 660 Ghana cedis per bag. In 2022/2023 it was 800 Ghana cedis. The average cocoa farmer produces about 5 to 12 bags of cocoa every year. This is about 4,000 to 10,000 Ghana cedis annually. That used to be a lot of money but when a tiny piece of gold can fetch 1,000 Ghana cedis the cocoa income reduces in value. A small-scale illegal miner can make in a week what the cocoa farm generates in a year. It is therefore understandable why a young man will rather go into illegal mining than go into farming. Also, if a miner can pay about 50,000 Ghana cedis for an acre of land the cocoa farmer will sell the farm than wait for that amount of money in a decade.

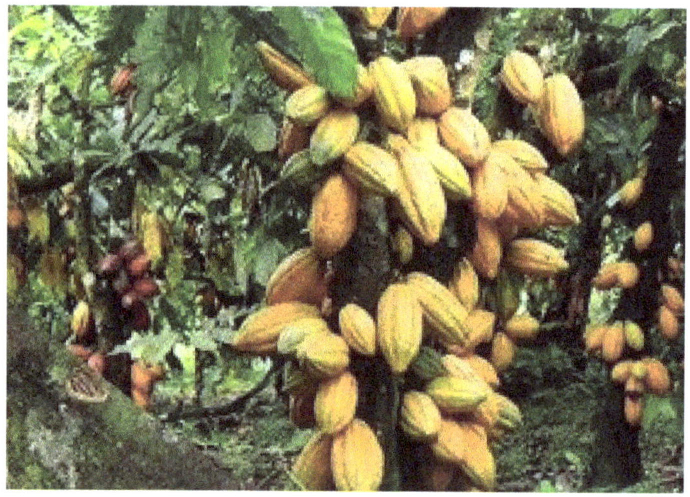

Cocoa

Every type of illegal mining has its price which is paid by the citizens of the country. The surface mining routinely destroys a larger part of the land especially when bulldozers are used to remove the fertile topsoil. The multinationals remove about 100 million tons of topsoil for just about 0.3 grams of gold. The illegal miners rent bulldozers and work all day removing the topsoil to cover cost. When the cost of renting and operating the bulldozer far exceeds the profits, they abandon the site and move to a different location leaving behind moonscape land. The land is not reclaimed and so nothing can be done in that location. It cannot be used for any kind of farming. It also becomes a trap for the people in the vicinity. If your farmlands happen to be beyond the Galamsey site, then it becomes very dangerous or worse impossible to get to your farm.

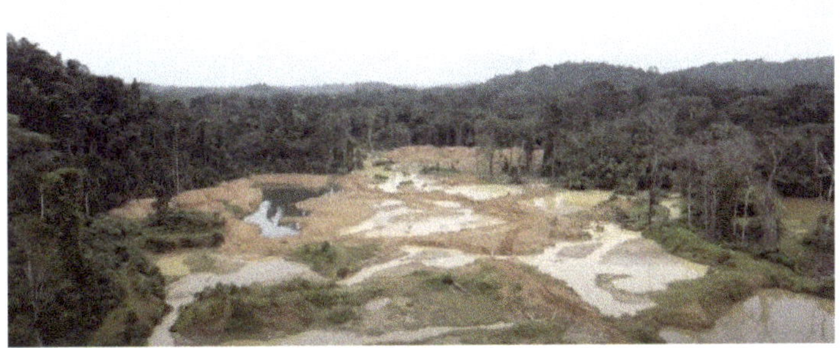

Abandoned Mining Site

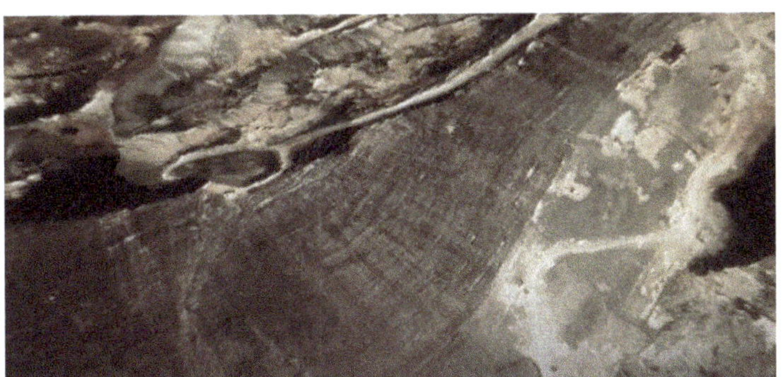

Arial view of Tarkwa Gold Mines

The farmers cannot be wholly blamed for selling their lands. There are factors beyond their control. If the land is given out for legal small-scale farming, then the farmer is limited to accepting a meager compensation. Such a farmer will have no other means to survive and will have to join the illegal trade. If a farmer's neighbors sell their lands, then his situation is like checkmate in a game of chess. He will be sandwiched between miners and his land will in a short time be polluted and unfit for farming. He may not even get access to his farm if the entrances to his farm are full of holes. The worst part is if the miners decide to mine on his farm at night when he is sleeping. His only option will be to sell.

Mining has degraded once fertile lands in Ghana. The use of toxic heavy metals and acids, especially mercury and cyanide, has caused a massive habitat loss for a diversity of flora and fauna. Flora is the plant life such as flowers, fungi and microbes. Fauna is the animal life including wild and undiscovered animals. Flora and fauna depend on each other. Destroying one means destroying both as one cannot survive without the other. Mining unfortunately destroys both. Mining on any land makes it impossible to start a new farm on it. The nutrients needed by any farm crop are in the topsoil, but this is removed during the mining process. In the few places where the land is reclaimed, the chemicals applied during mining make the land unsuitable for any kind of farming. The bush fallow system requires farmlands to be left for a period of one to three years to recoup its nutrients. With mining the land will need a whole generation to recoup its nutrients.

The mining menace has led to soil compaction in these mining areas causing a reduction in nutrients and fertility. Soil compaction occurs when the soil particles are pressed together reducing the pore space between them. Mining removes the topsoil and all the vegetation that is essential to sustain ecological communities in Ghana. The illegal mining has also created soil erosion and degradation of lands adjacent to these mining sites. The mining activity on the land has led to sedimentation and contamination of the nearby water bodies. There is no study done regarding the effect of mining on animals in the country but there is clear evidence that species of vertebrate are threatened.

Part 11.13 - No small-scale gold minor shall use explosives in his operations.

Small--Scale Gold Mining Law, 1989 – PNDCL 218

Chapter 5

Effects of Galamsey on the Air Quality

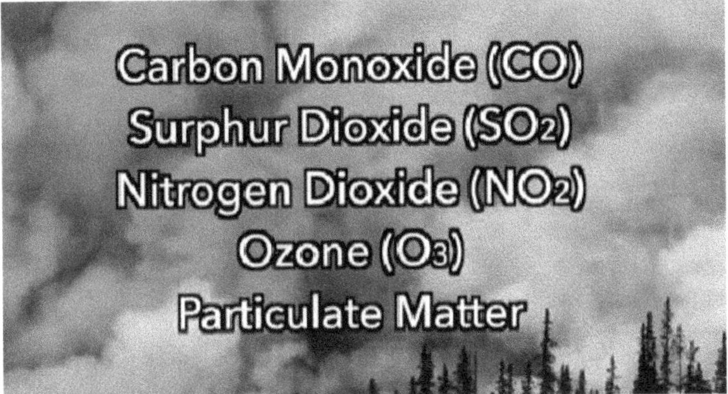

There are different methods used in measuring air quality in different countries. Air quality is basically a measure that shows if the air is clean or polluted. It is measured with the Air Quality Index (AQI). The air quality measure monitors the levels of pollutants in the atmosphere. AQI tracks five major air pollutants namely the Ground Level Ozone, Carbon Monoxide, Sulfur Dioxide, Nitrogen Dioxide and Airborne Particles (or Aerosols). According to the World Health Organization

(WHO), 99 per cent of the global population breathes unclean air.

Ghana like many other developing countries do not have the means to provide enough air monitoring stations across the country. On October 14, 2021, the United States of America (USA) Ambassador to Ghana inaugurated an air quality monitoring station on the US Embassy grounds in Cantonments, Accra. This became the third air monitoring station in Accra.

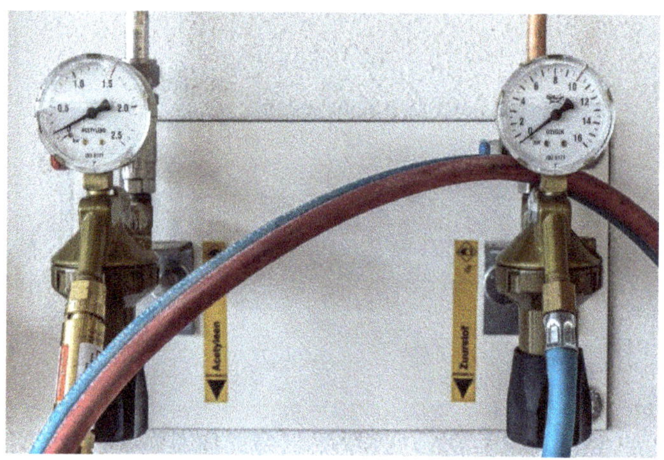

Monitoring Air Quality

The Environmental Protection Agency (EPA) with the support of the World Bank had previously installed two other air monitoring systems at the University of Ghana, Legon campus and at the St. Joseph's Roman Catholic

Basic School in Adabraka also in Accra. There are no systems to monitor the air quality in the mining areas where they are urgently needed. The quality of the air in these mining areas can only be deduced from the several reported health cases.

Air quality is negatively affected in every stage of the mining process and has a significant impact on the health of both the miners and the people in surrounding communities. Mining in Ghana can be classified as underground or above ground. Both above ground and underground mining processes produce enough air pollutants that generate harmful aerosols. Particulate Matters (PM) and Methane (CH4) gas emissions are the causes of a greater part of air pollution in these mining activities. Irresponsible mining has led to the destruction of climate protecting trees. Most miners do not have the knowledge of the precise locations of the gold deposits and move from one mining site to the next in search of the illusive strike. This has led to the removal of large surface areas of the vegetation that is supposed to protect the environment. In addition to the vast amount of dust, various harmful gases are also emitted into the atmosphere from the chemical reaction of the use of explosives and mining equipment.

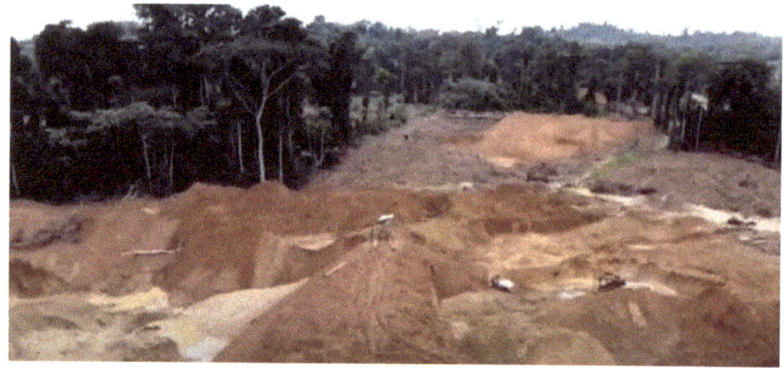

Tano Nimiri Forest Reserve

The use of excavators in illegal mining to clear these large surface areas causes erosion and unrefined materials from the sites become airborne. These airborne materials contain chemicals such as Carbon monoxide (CO), Carbon dioxide (CO2), Nitrogen (N2), Nitrogen dioxide (NO2) and Sulfur dioxide (SO2), which are very harmful to the environment. Carbon monoxide (CO) is a poisonous, colorless, odorless gas which is harmful and sometimes fatal when inhaled. Carbon dioxide (CO2) is the primary carbon source for life on earth. Too much concentration in the atmosphere has a devastating consequence. This gas is released during the combustion processes of the heavy machines used in illegal mining. Nitrogen (N2) is a gas that makes most of the air we breathe. Too much of it has a negative effect on humans such as irritation of the eyes, nose and throat. It causes reduced lung function, coughing, wheezing and shortness of breath. Nitrogen dioxide (NO2) is another highly toxic gas or pollutant caused by the emissions of mining equipment. Nitrogen dioxide levels monitoring is essential for any good ventilation design of all deep underground mines. Apart from effects on human health, it decreases plant growth and causes lower crop yield. It also creates loss of plant diversity in mining areas and increase in algal growth in aquatic ecosystems. Sulfur dioxide (SO2) is also toxic and high levels have a life-threatening effect. It causes burning of both the nose and throat, breathing difficulties and severe airway destruction.

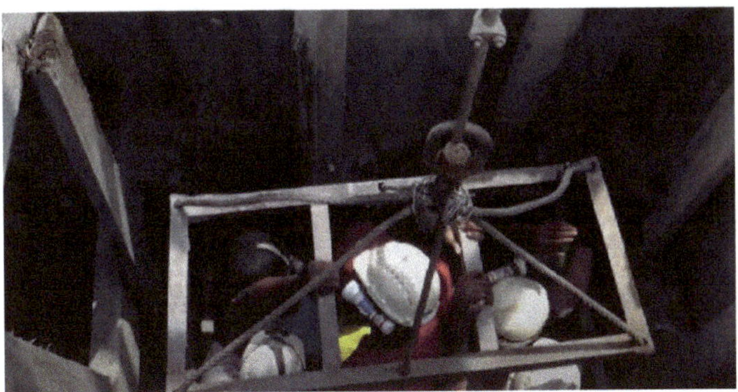

Underground Pit

Gases released during mining activities have negative effects on the health of both the mining workers and people living near the mining sites. Respiratory problems are caused by the exposure to these respiratory pollutants but most of these miners ignore the initial symptoms and seek medical treatment only when their situation is acute, and it is too late.

The effect of air quality is more precarious in the underground pits than in surface mining. The large-scale mining companies have some form of air quality monitoring systems and have limits on the duration a worker can stay underground. Unfortunately, the illegal small-scale miner working in a hazardous abandoned underground pit that is no longer used by the original owners cannot afford any monitoring device. There is no regulation on the number of hours or even days one can spend underground. It is left to the miner to test his endurance. Some miners spend a few hours, but a few greedy ones spend days and even weeks in these dark holes. They come out when they are not able to endure the pain any longer. During their stay in these dark underground pits, they breathe the polluted air filled with toxic gases from these mining activities. The pit tunnel is very narrow, and the working space underground is barely big enough to allow them to work. The toxic gases have no way of escaping and poison the working areas. It is a horrible way to make a living but since there are no alternative means of supporting their families, they must go through the ordeal.

Gases that are released during these mining activities are the main occupational hazards. Exposure to respiratory pollutants takes some time to manifest, making these miners ignore the initial symptoms. They are more concerned with actual injuries from blasts and collapsed caves than with respiratory diseases. The true measure is the number of newly diagnosed kidney and other respiratory damage as well as sudden death among the youth, especially those engaged in mining. Until the government can conduct a good survey the true scale of the destruction of human resources due to mining will remain unknown. In a more developed nation where civil suit of miners is possible, miners are not able to do irresponsible mining. In a developing country like Ghana, no one is held accountable, and no compensation is paid to those bearing the brunt of this havoc.

There are very good practices to control the air quality in mining areas and must be mandated by the supervising authorities and the government. If mining is done in a proper way, they can introduce dust suppression such as mist sprayers and wet drilling. These can be done at the loading, transfer and unloading points. Wind screens can be used to restrain dust particles. Water sprinkler vehicles can be used to regularly water the exposed surfaces. Regular vehicle and machine maintenance can also help reduce pollution. These may seem simple but someone doing illegal mining is not going to spend money on any of them.

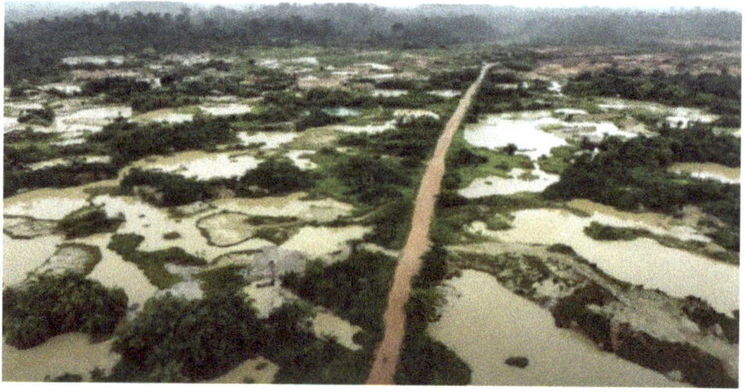

Mining along a road.

Air pollution from irresponsible mining has a very real impact on the lives of these miners as well as those in the surrounding communities. The way out of this impasse is the creation of jobs for the youth. The use of brute force has not been an effective deterrent.

Part 11.15 - For a period of three years from the date of the coming into force of this Law, all persons engaged in small-scale gold mining operations shall be exempted from the payment of income tax and royalties in respect of such mining operations.

Small--Scale Gold Mining Law, 1989 – PNDCL 218

Chapter 6
Effects of Galamsey on the People

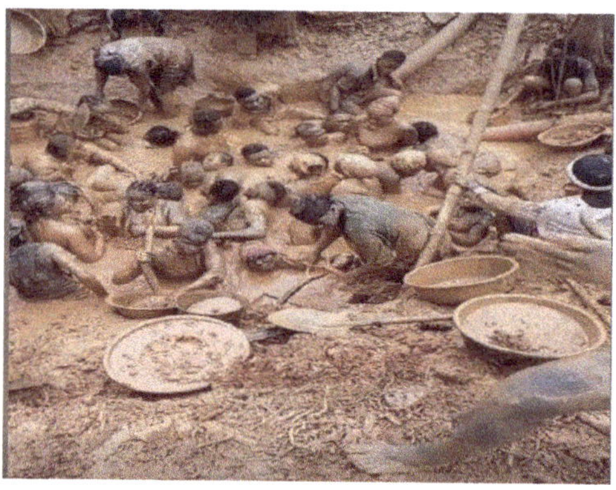

The full effects of the mining menace on the people are yet to be revealed. Ghana is a developing country, and more than half of the citizens depend on the land and rivers to make a living. Those that do not directly make a living from the land and the rivers rely on them for their drinking water and staple foodstuffs. Unfortunately, the land, the rivers and the atmosphere are poisoned by these miners. The chemicals used by the miners are eventually passed on to the people. There are some effects that are quite visible and felt by the citizens now, others are yet to manifest.

The World Bank describes the small-scale mining sector as an important income source for the local population of developing countries such as Ghana. In a country where good paying jobs are hard to come by, the mining sector has ensured the existence of millions of families in the rural areas. It has also contributed to the production of high demand minerals in the world. These miners contribute a great deal to their local economies. Unlike the multinationals, all the income of local miners stays and sustains their local economy. Without these mining jobs, most of the people, especially the youth, will be unemployed. Mining offers direct and indirect employment to mostly unskilled workers in the rural areas. The small-scale mining sector contributed close to 7 per cent of the gold revenue in Ghana in 2002. These miners contribute to building schools, clinics and sometimes roads in their local communities. Some even provide power plants and help in other developments in these rural areas. These development projects are the reasons it is very difficult to stop these miners from operating in these local communities. These necessities are supposed to be provided by the central government but unfortunately the resources of the country are not enough to reach many of the rural communities.

These miners rely on the locals to provide their basic supplies, especially the provision of breakfast, lunch and supper at the mining sites. Local small businesses blossom near these mining sites. The miners fortunately have the money so the locals sell anything that a miner going underground for a few days will need. Local small petrol stations spring up along the road to the mining sites. Motorcycle (Okada) operators provide the means to transport these miners to sites which are sometimes far away with no proper roads. All these indirect jobs will disappear if the fight to stop illegal mining is successful. The negative impact of the irresponsible mining on the environment however far outweighs the benefits of jobs for the local people.

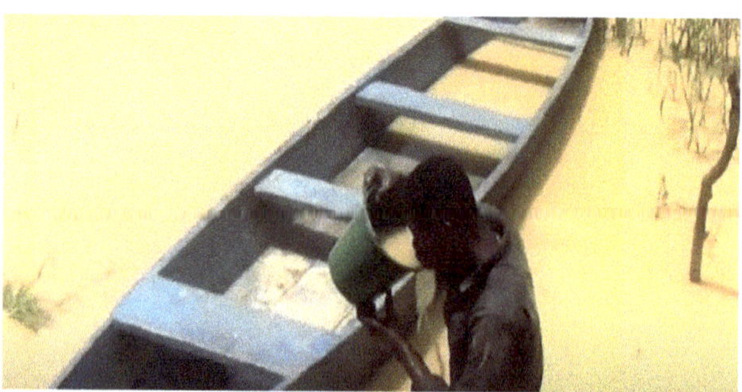

Drinking from the river.

Good clean drinking water and quality air are essential for healthy living. Ghanaians in the cities and big towns rely on pipe borne water and those in the rural areas rely on the rivers and streams. Unfortunately, these legal and illegal miners have polluted all the rivers in the country. The use of mercury and cyanide, which negatively affects the nervous system, is a major concern. This has led to the need to buy purified bottled or sachet water both in the cities and rural areas. This is quite expensive for people with a minimum income.

A report of the Population and Housing Census in 2021 listed the literacy rate in Ghana at 69.8 per cent. This is quite high and enviable compared to the nearby countries. Unfortunately, the activity of illegal mining is attracting these young school children and keeping them away from the classroom. There is the risk of truancy and school dropout in these mining communities. This will affect the impressive literacy rate Ghana has enjoyed since independence. Children are easily swayed by the opulence displayed by these illegal miners. They end up joining them with little persuasion and money. Only those kids with strong family supervision stay away from this magnetism.

The health effects of illegal mining are not yet fully known. It is however known that more people die from collapsed underground pits than any other form of mining. Since these miners have limited engineering background, they create structures they believe are strong enough to support the underground operations. A little tremor and the whole structure caves in on them. Most of these accidents go unnoticed and the few that are reported cannot be saved because it will endanger the rescuers. Another major problem with underground pits is poor ventilation. These miners do not have any machines to monitor the oxygen and carbon dioxide levels underground. They continuously inhale poisonous air in these underground pits. Ghana never had a lot of reported cases of problems affecting the liver, kidney and nervous systems. These are now common in most of the mining areas. Clinics are also filled with all kinds of injuries resulting from mining accidents. In areas where a single pit is claimed by different groups, each group will blast their section without any regard to the safety of others in various parts of the pit. This has caused a lot of avoidable severe injuries.

The main activity in the rural areas is farming. Every family has a cocoa farm and various farms for basic foodstuff needs. Some farmlands have been sold to the miners. Almost all miners do not reclaim the land.

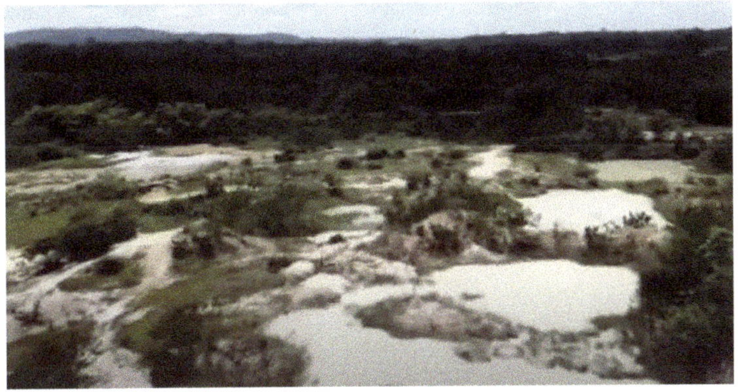

Destroyed farmland.

After creating numerous holes, the land becomes a wasteland post mining. A few strong-willed farmers who refuse to sell their farmlands are also blocked as the way to their farms is mined. Apart from the destruction of the land there is also no good source of water for anyone farming. A few rich farmers use irrigation for their farming activities, especially for rice farming. Irrigated farms are very few in Ghana. Since these rivers are polluted with chemicals, it is useless spending the little savings to construct inland irrigated waterways.

River fishing used to be the main source of fresh fish for most rural communities in Ghana. Most farmers always had basket fish traps in the rivers which they checked before coming home each day. The younger ones used the hook and line, and the professional fishermen used the cannon to do commercial fishing. River fishing is now futile in Ghana. The rivers are so polluted it is a miracle some fish still stay alive in them. The application of mercury and cyanide is killing the rivers. There is the problem of Bioaccumulation and Biomagnification. Bioaccumulation is the buildup of toxins within the individual organism, in this case the fish. Biomagnification is the buildup of these toxins as they move up the food chain. The big fish eat the smaller fish and humans eat the big fish with these harmful toxins.

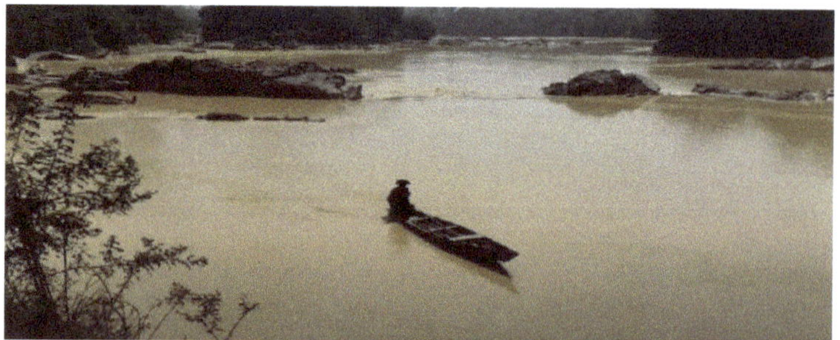

River Fishing.

Currently, there is no clinical data to assess the contamination in the community. The color of the rivers and the moonscape landscape are enough to point to a dangerous trend in the way the natural resources are being dissipated. Unemployment has been a problem in most developing countries. Ghana is not immune from this phenomenon. The main source of employment in the rural areas is farming. Since both the land and the river bodies are now destroyed, it is going to create more unemployment and food shortages crisis for the country.

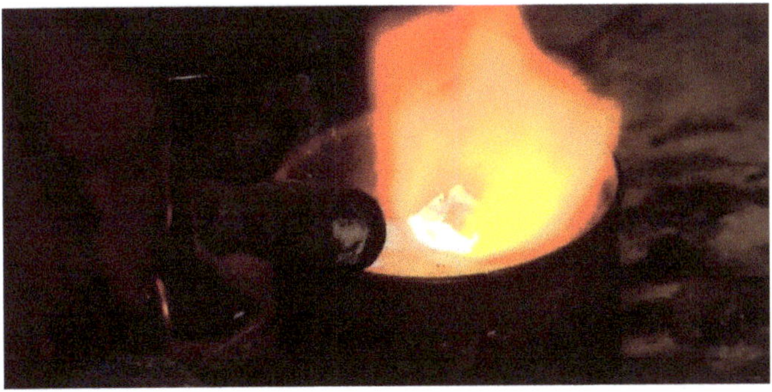

Burning Gold Mercury Amalgam

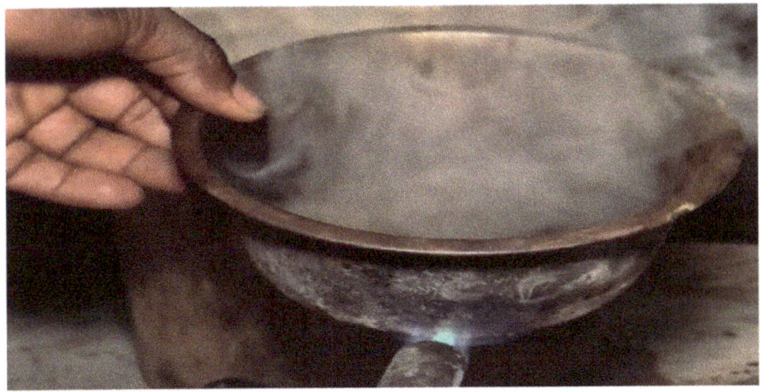

Mercury Vapor.

Gold dealers inadvertently poison their local communities. They purchase the gold mercury amalgam from the miners and extract the gold by heating up the gold mercury amalgam. An amalgam is an alloy of mercury with another metal. The gold dealers extract the gold by heating the gold mercury amalgam to vaporize the mercury leaving behind the gold. The poisonous mercury vapor is released into the neighborhood causing health problems for the whole community. The gold dealers bear the brunt of the health hazard, especially those heating the metals in enclosed environments.

The sad story of the remains of Baby X at the Kwame Nkrumah University of Science and Technology (KNUST) with extra limbs and no genitals is a warning to the country of the seriousness of the mining hazards. The reported cases of deformed unborn babies in these mining centers and placentae with heavy concentration of lead, mercury and arsenic can all be attributed to the emergence of irresponsible mining. There is no other way to explain why Ghana is having dysmorphic unborn babies with the autopsies showing high levels of these harmful poisonous chemicals.

Part 111.16 - Without prejudice to any enactment empowering any person or body to purchase and deal in gold, the Secretary may in consultation with the Minerals Commission in writing, license such persons as he may consider fit, to buy and deal in such types and forms of gold and under terms and conditions as may be specified in the license.

Small--Scale Gold Mining Law, 1989 – PNDCL 218

Chapter 7
Galamsey And Politics

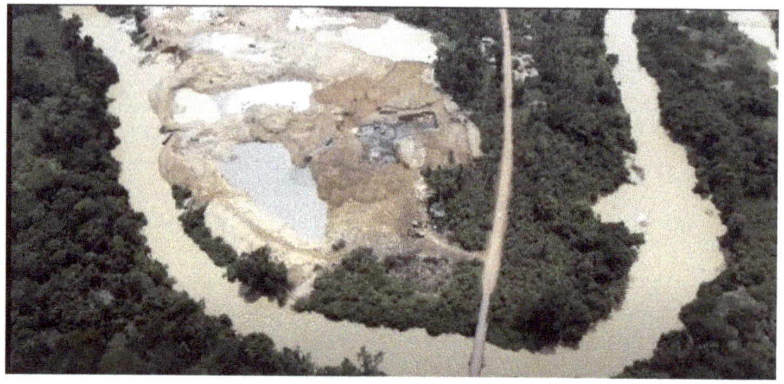

Mining next to river Tano.

The form of government practiced in Ghana is parliamentary democracy with an executive president. Elections are held every four years to usher in a new government. This democratic dispensation is very young and fragile. After a long period of military interferences there has been stability since 1992. This may seem to be the ideal climate for development in a small developing African country. The main problem with the kind of democracy practiced in Ghana is that it is a winner takes all system. The President makes all appointments after elections and if it is not a continuing government then it is likely almost all top government appointees will be replaced. That is the sad reality of democracy in Ghana. It is not surprising therefore that the main job of the main opposition party is to oppose every policy of the ruling government and portray it in a negative way.

Illegal mining negatively affects every citizen, irrespective of the political party affiliation. Galamsey is something every citizen was supposed to help find a remedy. Unfortunately, if a political party is not in government their members go round mining sites convincing the miners that when they come to power, they will allow them to work without any harassment. They also use every means to convince the miners that the ruling government is not allowing them to make a living because they harass them. In most developing countries, it takes very little to sway the minds of voters. The miners form a large group of the voting population, so such tactics of the opposition do work in changing governments. The sad part is that when the opposition political party is voted into power, they become the ones trying to find solutions to the mining menace.

Every government has tried to form a committee or task force to fight illegal and irresponsible mining.

When these task forces start working there are initial successes and obvious fruitful changes. Most of these task forces engage in seizing and sometimes burning mining equipment. A lot of the miners are usually arrested in the initial operations of the task force. After a short period, the people start to agitate because their machines are being seized and sometimes destroyed. They become unemployed and unable to provide for their families. They become bitter especially when they notice some of their colleagues still working. The main tool used to frustrate the task force is to accuse them of corruption. When a task force is tagged as corrupt, they immediately become ineffective. They spend all their time untangling themselves from the corruption tag. In most developing countries, people do not need to provide any evidence to accuse anyone of corruption. The onus is on the accused to prove that he is not corrupt.

When excavators are seized, they are often sent to the nearby Assembly Office. This is because the country does not have any other well-protected places to send them. The paper trail is often poor. Owners who know people in high places are easily able to get their equipment back as soon as they are seized. With time there is a discrepancy between the number of machines seized and the number at the storage facilities. Before there is any official statement there is always a huge uproar in the country about missing excavators. Some of the machines genuinely get lost in the system. Since some of these mining sites are owned by powerful people, it is not surprising that these machines are seized and released immediately. The equipment for some miners follows the "catch and release" policy. That is unfortunately the sad reality. Besides the machines, miners who are arrested are often released immediately and end up at the same sites where they were arrested. This gives credence to the fact that some of the miners work for powerful people.

Conducting elections every four years hinders a government's effectiveness in initiating stringent measures to fight the mining menace. In fighting the problem, the government must also think about the upcoming elections. Using excessive force alienates the miners who form a large part of the voting bloc. Any solution needs to be a balance between using force and appeasement. The government communicators are sent to explain issues on various radio and tv stations. Unfortunately, these measures are not enough as the opposition political parties are also invited for alternative views on these stations. Since all these stations lean towards a political party, they allow people to get away with spreading half-truths and propaganda. Some hosts even ask leading questions to enable the opposition to damage the ruling government and vice versa. With the emergence of social media, the fight against illegal mining has turned into replaying utterances of leading political party members on issues. It is difficult to promise the miners during election campaign and then use brute force when you are in power to fight them.

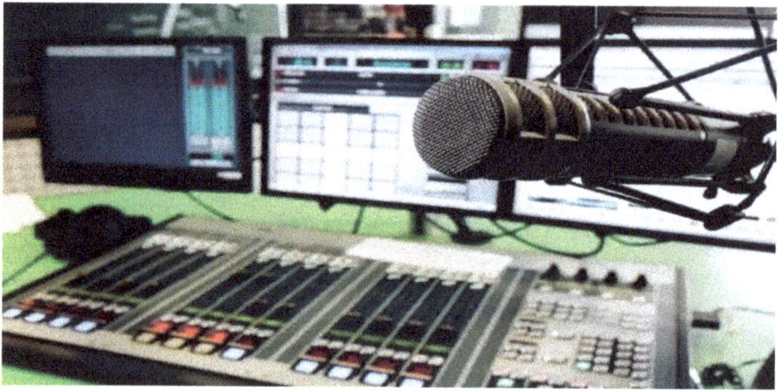

Illegal mining is a business with obscure mining site owners. The way the radio and tv stations allow some views on their platforms suggests complicity on their part. It is very difficult to know the true owners of these mining sites. The best way to hinder any initiative in the country is to turn it into politics. Illegal mining was something that most of the citizens were eager to see a permanent solution. The media spearheaded a campaign to fight it. Just when the rivers were returning to normality and the mining sites were getting reclaimed the energy fizzled out. It became obvious that some people were able to continue with their mining activities whilst others were stopped and even lost their equipment. The fight against illegal mining has become a major political issue in the country. Each political party uses the fight as a political tool to undermine the opposite political party. Whatever measures are introduced by the ruling political party are condemned vociferously by the opposition parties. This creates the real atmosphere for the ruling party to lose any upcoming elections.

There is no denying that mining is causing havoc in the country. Unfortunately, these miners have now become major financiers of some politicians. They provide both financial and logistical support during the busy election period. This makes it very difficult for these politicians to openly advocate for the total ban of these irresponsible mining. They may say in public that they are against any form of illegal mining, but their actions are opposite what they say in public. Politicians have similar characteristics all over the world. They toe the line of their political party. When they are in power, they are always explaining the effective policies they have implemented in fighting illegal mining. When they are out of government, they do not see any good policies implemented by the government in the fight against illegal mining. The two major political parties in the country have tasted power. Fortunately, they both tried the use of force to stop the illegal mining menace. Both parties recognized the destructive nature of the way mining was done.

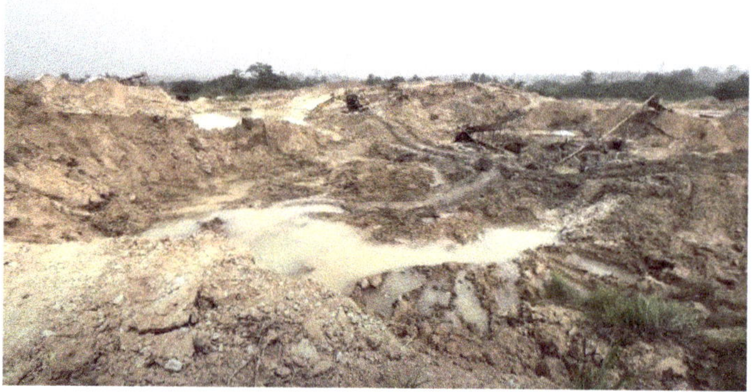

Wasteland

The problem with politicians is that they are very sensitive to the political cost of coming up with stringent measures that will turn the voters against them. It is clear any government that will completely stop illegal mining and be able to get all these miners to lay down their tools, will not be in power after the next general elections. No government can provide jobs for all the youth in a country. The best way is for the government to provide an enabling environment for the private sector to create jobs. The fight against illegal mining seems to be elusive. Until all the gold reserves in the country are depleted the canker will continue to be an albatross around the neck of every government. Since the blame will always be on the ruling government, the opposition party will continually use it as a political tool to undermine the government. Those in charge are not giving meaningful answers to genuine questions such as the whereabouts of missing excavators. Those not in government are fabricating stories and accusing the government. The Political games of the politicians with an issue that is destroying a country is very nauseating. Unfortunately, that is the sad situation in Ghana. What gives credence to the fact that the politicians do not care is how Parliament passed the controversial L.I. 2462 when the country had a mining crisis. L.I. 2462 "Environmental Protection (Mining in Forest Reserves) Regulation" allowed miners to mine in parts of reserved forests.

Part 111.17.(1) - Any licensed small-scale gold miner or any person in possession of gold may sell such gold in his possession to authorized buyers only.

Small--Scale Gold Mining Law, 1989 – PNDCL 218

Chapter 8

Galamsey And Chieftaincy

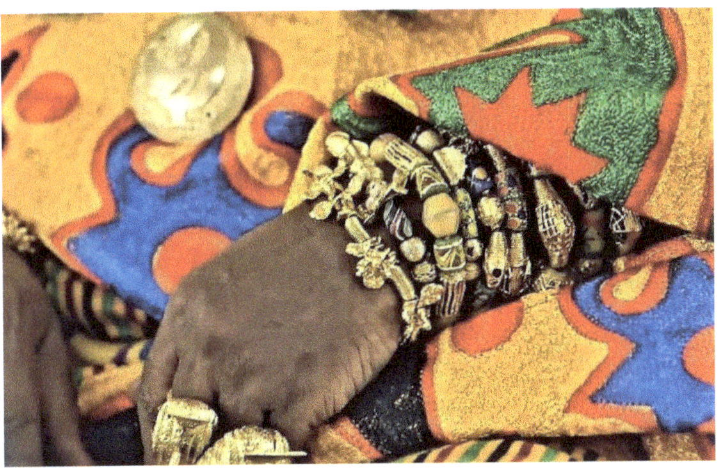

The land tenure system in Ghana is managed by a pluralistic legal system. Customary and statutory tenure systems overlap. Most of the land is under customary tenure and vested in chiefs. Chieftaincy is one of the oldest institutions in the country. It is recognized in the Ghana constitution as part of the governance system. Chiefs are the custodians of customs and traditions. They settle local disputes and govern the community lands. This means to acquire land in Ghana, you often must go through the traditional system. The constitution of Ghana states that every mineral in its natural state in, under and upon the land, rivers, streams, watercourses throughout the country is vested in the President of Ghana in trust of the people. The granting of mining license is therefore the sole prerogative of the state or government. The small-scale miner will complete all the mining processes with the Minerals Commission and Forestry Commission. After being granted a license, the miner moves to the mining site. Sometimes they pay a visit to the nearby chief who is the owner of the land out of curtesy.

There have been appeals to the government to engage chiefs in the fight against illegal mining. It is believed that since chiefs are not subjected to any four-year election cycle, they are not at risk of losing any power due to genuinely fighting Galamsey. Politicians on the other hand cannot be too firm in fighting illegal mining because it is the same miners who will be voting at the next general elections. There is a lot of blame on the chiefs and opinion leaders in these mining areas. It is believed their actions and inactions have led to the impunity with which illegal miners cause so much destruction. It is perplexing that miners can bring big, heavy mining equipment, especially excavators and chanfang machines to work in a community without the knowledge of the chiefs. The devastation is often too clear for all to observe and be concerned. It is difficult to see such destruction happen on the blind side of the chiefs, elders, assemblymen and the local people.

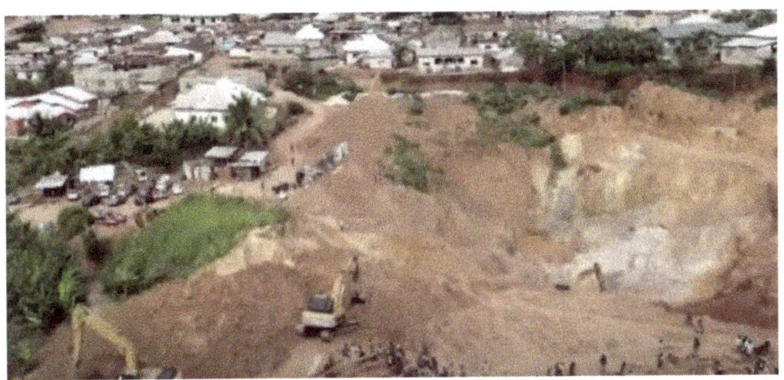

Mining next to a town.

Some chiefs in Ghana used to have their own police force in their palaces. They used to be called *Ahenfie* Police (Palace Police). They carried out executive and judicial functions in their towns and cities. These are, however, not the forces that can stop illegal mining. Illegal mining is big, risky business in Ghana with connections in high places. They also have some form of security who carry guns. They are ready to use force when their operations are threatened. The chiefs and people in the community are therefore powerless to stop a well-protected mining operation. The chiefs will be able to report the activities of illegal miners in their area to the authorities, but they cannot use any kind of force to stop their operations. If they are given a role in the granting of a mining license, they may be able to have a say in the approval process.

Most people go into illegal mining due to unemployment and greed. There is so much youth unemployment in the country pushing them to do illegal mining. Most of the chiefs in the country rule in areas where the youth cannot find work, making it difficult for them to completely advocate for a total ban on any form of mining. Some chiefs blame the politicians for the uptick in illegal mining activities. They claim most of the miners are protected by powerful men. This may be due to the lack of arrests when these miners are reported to the authorities. The few that are arrested to make a political statement are released immediately after they are arrested. This gives credence to the fact that most of the miners have powerful people protecting them. It is even believed some of the concessions belong to the powerful people and the miners are just their workers.

Most of the policies geared towards ending the illegal mining menace have been to involve the security agencies to use force on these miners. It has therefore become the accepted norm that only force can be used to fight illegal mining. Since chiefs do not have any control over the security agencies, they have remained passive onlookers expecting the security agencies to fight the canker. No chief will risk his life to go and ask illegal miners to leave his land. For fear of losing the respect they have, they will ignore the problem and keep quiet. It is even worse when these miners are protected by armed security. Mining is a risky business and wherever there is money at stake people act in aggressive ways.

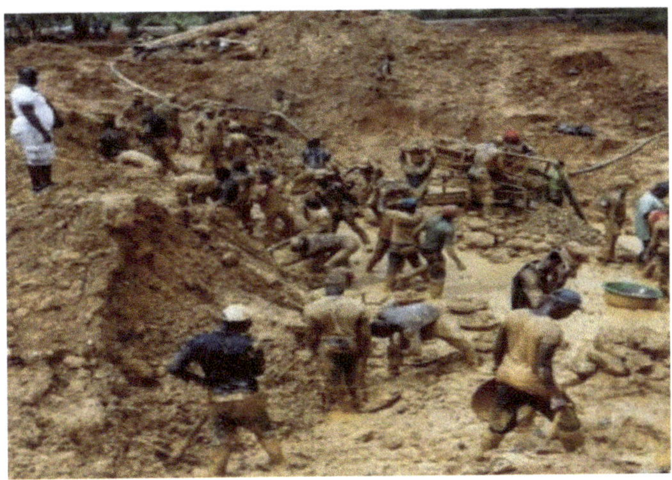

In most rural communities, the land does not belong to the chief. Most of the land is family inherited.

If a family decides to sell their small piece of land they own to illegal miners because they are going to receive instantly an amount that is equivalent to what they will receive in two or three decades the chief will not be able to stop it. The chief only has control over the stool land, but the bulk of the land is in the hands of individual families. When individuals are making a lot of money selling their lands, it would be naive to think the chief will be able to resist attempts to influence him with money from the miners. It is said one person does not rule. Even if the chief is strong willed, the people around him cannot all be strong willed to resist mining money.

In many developing countries, the government provides most of the basic amenities such as schools, roads, pipe borne water and electricity. Since all developing countries are struggling to pay the huge interest on foreign loans and pay workers' salaries, rural areas are often left to fend for themselves. These miners have been able to provide some of these necessities. Some build schools and roads in their rural villages and towns. Others provide generators, power plants and bore holes. The chiefs and people in the areas where the miners contribute to their development will never ask the miners to stop their activities even though they are destroying the environment.

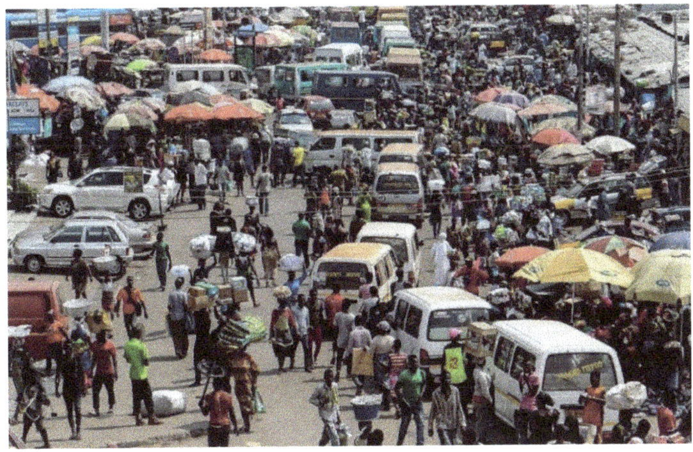

Booming Market

The main reason the youth engage in this risky business is the lack of good paying jobs for them after school. Except for a few greedy ones, most of these young people will not risk their lives if there is a better alternative. The Chiefs are aware of this problem that affects their youth. It is therefore important to know and understand why the chief will not try to stop the youth from mining. Mining has a way of falsely portraying a town as a booming economy. These miners spend all that they earn on their local economy. Those area sellers make good profits on these miners. Shops spring up to cater for the needs of these miners. Petrol sellers open small stations along the route to the mining sites. These are activities that will shut down if illegal mining is stopped. No chief would like his town or village to look like a ghost town after illegal mining is abolished.

Illegal mining kingpins are very rich. They can compromise almost anybody standing in the way of their activities. It is easy to blame chiefs and authorities but when these kingpins visit, they can grease the palms of people in a way that will make them turn the other way. Most of the mining activities occur in villages in the country. These chiefs are not rich even though they dress majestically. A lot of money to these chiefs is peanuts to the rich gold miner. Any amount of money to make a chief and his people happy can easily be donated by the miners. The chiefs are caught between a rock and a hard place when it comes to stopping illegal mining in their communities. A few chiefs have recently been de-stooled for allowing or engaging in Galamsey in their areas. It is however well known that some chiefs are linked to mining concessions.

Part 111.17.(2) - A person shall be presumed to be lawfully in possession of gold until the contrary is proved.

Small--Scale Gold Mining Law, 1989 – PNDCL 218

Chapter 9
Galamsey Measures Implemented

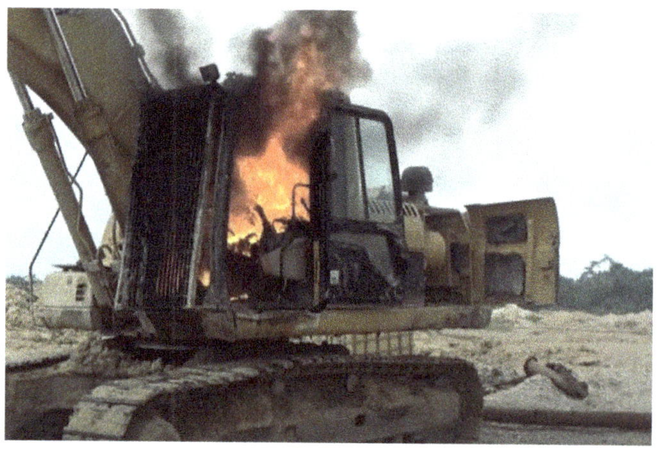

The battle to stop illegal mining has been ongoing since illegal mining started. Before illegal mining became a menace, the security agencies never bothered miners until there was a crime or complaint lodged against a miner. It was also not obvious to notice any area as having mining activity. With the advent of the menace, it became necessary for governments to act. Rivers were being destroyed beyond comprehension.

The once fertile farmlands were turned into moonscape surfaces. Ghana is a developing country implying most of the citizens depend on farming and fishing. The destruction of the rivers meant both city dwellers and villages needed to buy water for daily use (Bottled water and Sachet water). The main source of income used to be from cocoa farming. That is not the case anymore. These miners were buying good cocoa farms and turning them into mining sites. The land to plant basic staple food was being turned into wasteland making it unfit for any farming activity. The path to farms became dangerous with foot paths being blocked by mining activities. There was no other way out but for the government to act. The mining issues also became a political issue as each political party used it to discredit and undermine the ruling political party.

The Small-scale Mining Act (PNDL218) - The first attempt to curb the canker was in 1989. The government passed a law to legalize and regularize the small-scale mining sector by introducing a licensing process. The Small-scale Mining Act (PNDL218) was passed which was later integrated into the Mining Act 703 (2006). The act provided the blueprint for the sanitization and formalization of small-scale mining and reserved it solely for Ghanaians. This law enabled artisanal miners to apply for up to 25 acres of concession in designated areas through the Minerals Commission. The granting of mining license did not stop the destruction caused by illegal mining requiring successive governments to come up with other measures.

Operation Flush Out – In 2006 Operation Flush Out was launched to deal with the illegal mining issues. It was a nationwide military exercise to flush out illegal miners. The Minerals and Mining Act of 2006 (Act 703) was passed prohibiting foreign citizens from engaging in small-scale mining in the country. Operation Flush Out was aimed at disrupting the activities of illegal miners using the military service.

Inter-Ministerial Taskforce - In May 2013, a five-member inter-ministerial taskforce was inaugurated to fight illegal small-scale mining throughout the mining areas in the country. The responsibilities of the taskforce were to seize all the equipment the illegal miners use, arrest and prosecute both Ghanaians and non-Ghanaians engaged in small-scale illegal mining, deport all non-Ghanaians engaged in illegal small-scale mining and to revoke the license of any Ghanaian who sub-lease their concession to non-Ghanaian. They were also to hold Metropolitan, Municipal and District Chief Executives (MMDCE) and district security council accountable for any illegal mining activity in their areas of jurisdiction. In July that year, the taskforce reported that 1,568 foreigners and 51 Ghanaians were arrested, 40 vehicles, 85 earth moving equipment and 49 weapons were seized. They also reported that 3,877 foreigners, including those who submitted themselves voluntarily were deported.

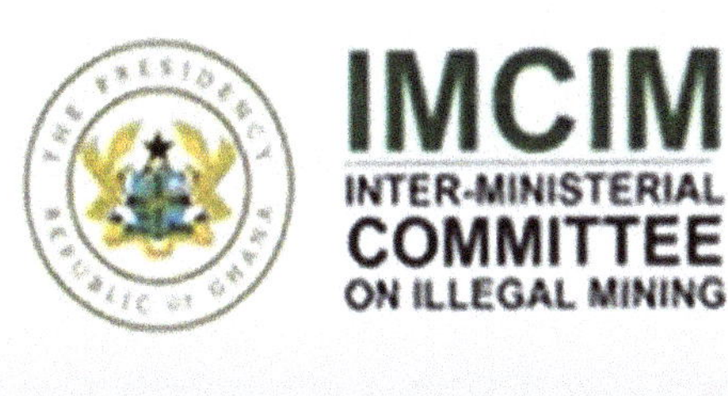

Inter-Ministerial Committee on Illegal Mining (IMCIM) - In March 2017 another committee known as the Inter-Ministerial Committee on Illegal Mining (IMCIM) was formed. The IMCIM was to bolster the existing stakeholder agencies related to artisanal and small-scale mining sectors such as the Minerals Commission, Environment Protection Agency, Water Resources Commission and Forestry Commission. The IMCIM was tasked to ensure that existing agencies enforced the existing laws, set up ad hoc district mining committees, vet and verify mining companies, sanitize and regularize small-scale mining activities, train Artisanal and Small-scale miners (ASM), reclaim degraded land and restore impacted water bodies, coordinate activities relating to alternative livelihoods for the youth. In 2021 the IMCIM was dissolved.

Six-month Ban - In April 2017 the government placed an initial six-month ban on artisanal and small-scale mining. The ban was extended many times to enable the government to fully sanitize the mining sector. The Chief Justice designated seven High Courts and seven Circuit Courts in Accra, Sekondi, Kumasi, Koforidua, Cape Coast, Bolgatanga and Sunyani to deal with mining cases. The Parliament also amended the Minerals and Mining Act to prescribe harsher sentences. The ban was lifted in December 2018, a year after it was placed. After the ban was lifted, all registered small-scale miners were asked to submit all mining documents to the Inter-Ministerial Committee on Illegal Mining for vetting before returning to their mining sites.

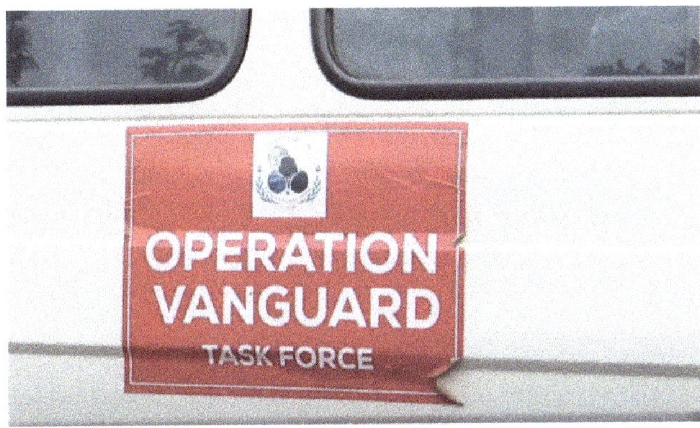

Operation Vanguard – In July 2017 Operation Vanguard was launched. It was a joint military and police taskforce of 400 personnel comprising 200 military and 200 police personnel. Three operating bases were established in the most ravaged regions in Ghana namely Ashanti, Eastern and Western regions. They were tasked to stay at their assigned areas until all forms of illegal mining stopped in those regions and all unauthorized mining pits permanently destroyed. Operation Vanguard was equipped with drones and included trained drone pilots.

Galamstop Taskforce - In 2019 a 62-member Galamstop taskforce was inaugurated to protect the Birim river. Members of this task force were trained in diving, swimming and other water techniques. They were equipped with speed boats to patrol the Birim river and its tributaries. The Galamstop taskforce was inaugurated to complement the efforts of Operation Vanguard.

Operation Halt - In April 2021 Operation Halt was launched. It was made up of personnel from the Ghana Armed Forces and Forestry Commission. The taskforce sought to remove all persons and mining equipment from water bodies and forest reserves in the country. Their tasks included decommissioning and demobilizing equipment where needed. In October 2022 Operation Halt was relaunched as **Operation Halt II** to reinforce the war on illegal mining. In the second phase the granting of mining licenses by the Minerals Commission involved the inputs of chiefs, regional ministers and district chief executives (MMDCEs)

The measures implemented so far have all been an initial success followed by the worsening of the mining destruction. They all had catchy names with a lot of hope to eliminate the canker. The fact that the menace is still ongoing means they did not achieve their main aims. Most of the measures involved using force to stop something that people were willing to sacrifice their lives in doing it. Physics taught us that when force is applied to any object it either moves or deforms. All the forces applied to stop illegal mining deformed the situation. In most cases it got the people angry not because force was being applied but because force was applied unfairly. The smaller miners were forced to stop working and the bigger well-connected miners were seen still operating. Even though some miners engage in this menace because of greed, most of them do it to survive. It is therefore hard to use force to stop someone engaging in any activity to survive. Another reason for the shortfall of these measures is the corruption tag. In a country where the corruption index is high it is very easy to have a task force reviled with a corruption tag.

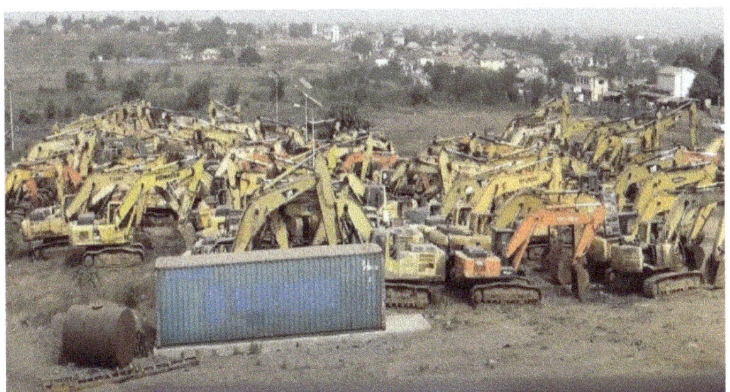

Seized Excavators

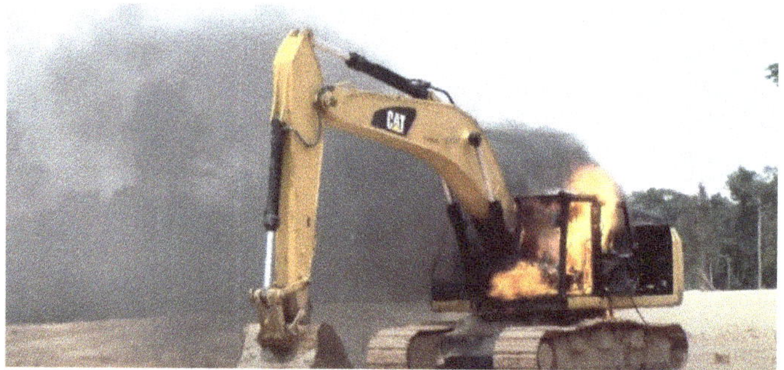

Burning Excavator

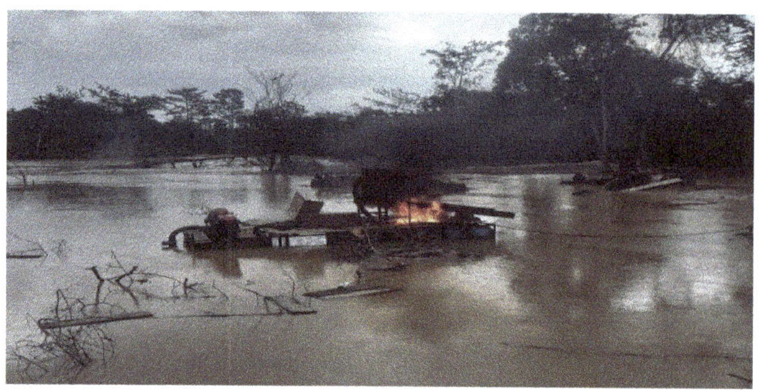

Burning Changfa Machine

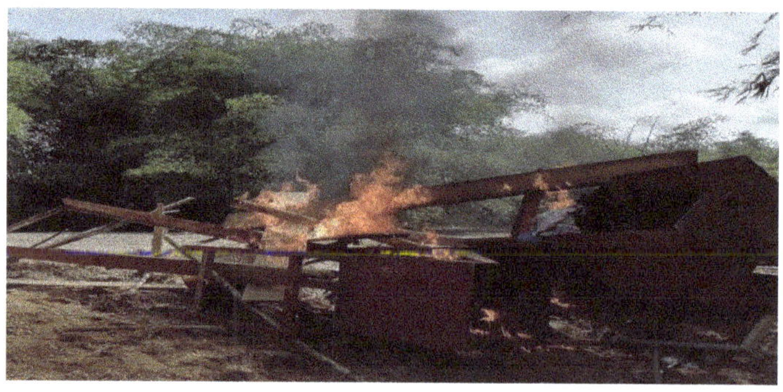

Burning Galamsey Site

There are many reasons these task forces failed to eliminate the illegal mining menace. These task forces lacked the necessary tools for the fight against illegal mining. They lacked logistics, had operational challenges and didn't work long enough to have a lasting impression. The suspicion of corruption discouraged the needed community support required in such a difficult fight. The involvement of powerful people in illegal mining made it unsafe for anyone trying to be a hero. In a developing country, if you become the face of the struggle to stop powerful people, you and your whole family pay the ultimate price for it. The most devastating part was the quick release of arrested miners and their machines. This gave credence to the perception that some of these miners were working for prominent people. It was evident some of the mining concessions were owned by very powerful people.

Part 111.18 - Nothing contained in this law or in any other enactment shall be construed as precluding any person from dealing with or disposing of his gold jewelry, gold artifact or gold coin to authorized dealers or to any person whatsoever.

Small--Scale Gold Mining Law, 1989 – PNDCL 218

Chapter 10

The Future of Galamsey

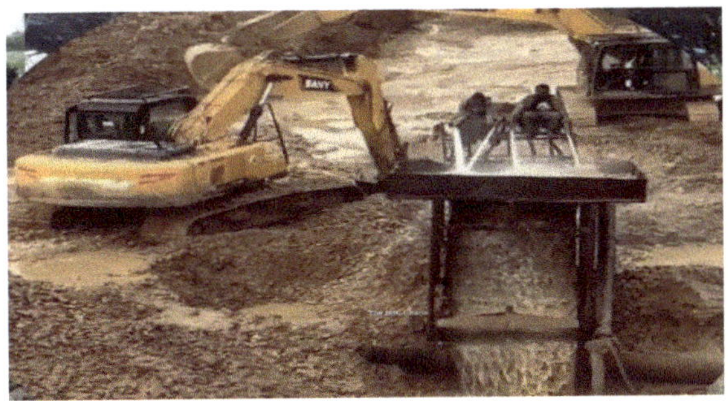

Gold has been extracted from Ghana since it was inhabited by our ancestors. It was not illegal to extract gold, and it was mainly for local consumption, particularly used by the chiefs. Gold is a heavy metal, so the average Ghanaian did not dress wearing too much gold. When the Europeans came and colonized the country the appetite for gold increased. The Europeans initially traded in these precious metals before their attention shifted to slave trading. Prospecting for gold never destroyed the rivers and farmlands even when large multinationals were given permits to mine. The illegal gold mining menace is a recent phenomenon, and it is hard to pinpoint the exact year that it started. The small-scale mining law had to be enacted in 1989 when it became obvious that too many people were mining irresponsibly and destroying the rich farmlands and rivers in the country.

In 1989 the small-scale mining law was enacted to sanitize the industry. This allowed every citizen interested in mining the opportunity to obtain a gold mining license and mine gold lawfully and responsibly in the country. The bottlenecks in obtaining a license have rendered most of the youth still engaged in illegal mining. The average rural Ghanaian youth cannot afford a gold mining license even if it is free. Most previous governments formed task forces to curb irresponsible mining. Mining license is not granted for mining in water bodies or 100 feet from the water bodies yet all the rivers in the country have suffered the same fate of illegal mining either in them or close to them. It is obvious that Ghana will need to find a new source of water in the very near future. These numerous force interventions have all failed to curb and control the harm done by illegal and irresponsible mining. It is still likely future governments will also form these task forces to fight illegal mining even though none of them really worked. Evidently, it is impossible to use brute force to control these miners. The miners need other measures to persuade them to stop this menace themselves.

The future of Galamsey will be determined by the availability of these precious minerals. These illegal miners are currently mining the minerals close to the surface. There are abundant reserves if they decide to dig deeper like the multinationals. If these precious gems are abundant in the country people from far and near will troop in to try to be rich before they die. There are so many reasons why illegal mining will continue into the very distant future. Unless the country can come up with solutions to the myriads of problems affecting the people, especially the youth, this canker will continue to destroy the air, land and rivers that are needed to sustain life. The cure is in the hands of the people, and they need to be offered a better livelihood before they give up this lifestyle that is destroying the country and their future.

All African countries face unemployment challenges. The unemployment rate in Ghana in 2023 was 3.60 percent according to the International Labor Organization (ILO). That is a very good rate, however it is quite misleading. There are no jobs in the country for the youth. It is therefore not surprising that the youth have all turned to illegal mining to survive.

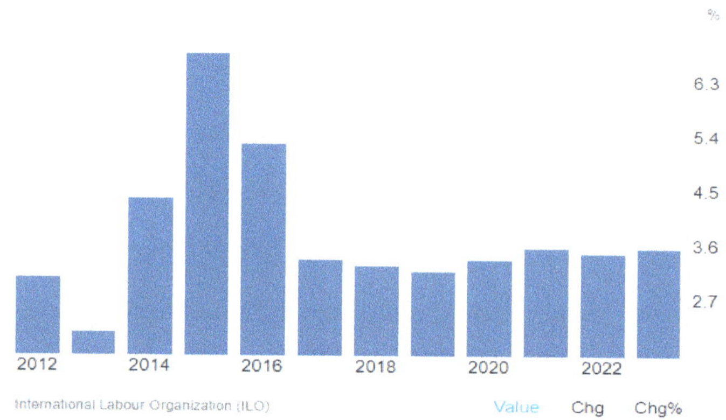

Ghana Unemployment Chart

The small-scale mining sector is now one of the main jobs for a vast majority of the population, especially the unskilled population. In May 2018, the government had to address the graduate unemployment in the country by launching the Nation Builders Corps (NaBCo). This was a scheme which hired 100,000 unemployed graduates when it was launched for a three-year period. Until the unemployment issue is permanently addressed the need to survive will drive people to find any available means.

The cities and big towns used to be the main attraction points for rural youth migration. That is not the case anymore. Mining sites have taken over as the main migration points for rural youth. They know the work is very dangerous, but they are willing to risk their lives for the illusive yellow dirt, gold. Farming and fishing were the main work in the small towns and villages. The emergence of irresponsible small-scale mining has deprived these towns of land to farm and rivers to fish. The only thing left for them to do is join the illegal mining sector. Any amount of money obtained from mining is enough to provide their daily meal and have extra to help other siblings and parents. These youth will risk injuries and death to make ends meet in a Galamsey pit.

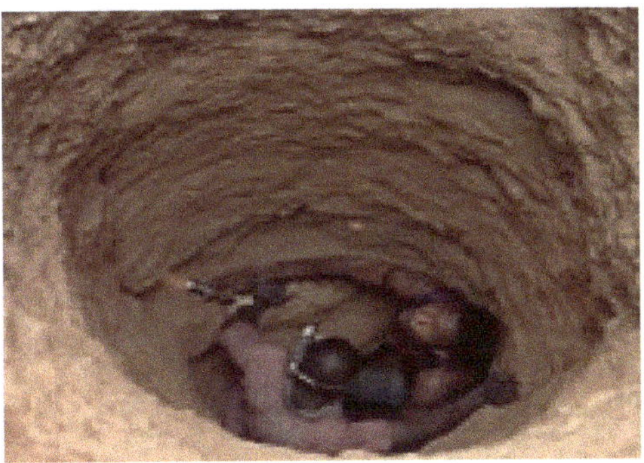

Gold Pit

The main cash crop in Ghana is cocoa. Almost every family except those in the big cities had a cocoa farm that provided all the money they needed for the whole year. There was enough money in cocoa farming to prevent youth in cocoa growing areas from migrating. They would rather stay in their rural communities and help with the farm work instead of migrating to the big towns and cities. With the emergence of gold mining, the cocoa farm has lost its value.

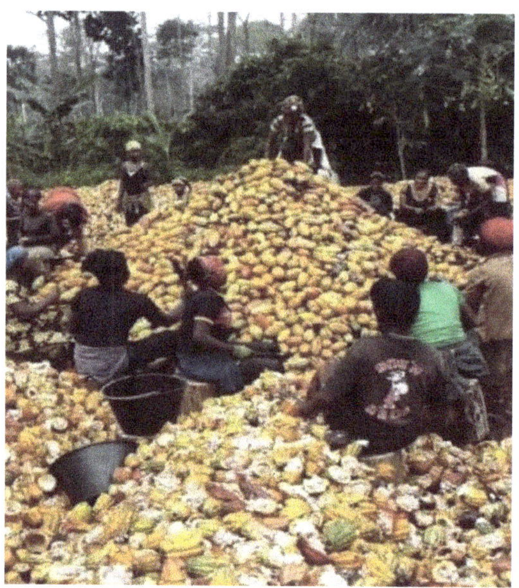

Harvesting cocoa.

The small-scale miner is now able to get in a week and sometimes in a day the amount of money a cocoa farm will generate in the year. The youth now prefer the get rich quick way of living than the cocoa farming that generates income only at the end of the cocoa season at the end of the year.

Greed has been a universal trait in the history of mankind. Some of the miners are not into mining to survive but are just greedy. Their greed is manifest in their desire to get as many mining sites as possible. If it is not greed, then no one needs more than one mining concession. The unending pursuit of wealth has driven the youth of the country to risk their lives in ways unimaginable. With the many dangers, injuries and pits collapsing regularly, these miners still engage in illegal mining. In many places having money also means having power. In developing countries, if you have money, you become more powerful than the leaders of the town or village. The days of being satisfied with a monthly paycheck are over. Everyone wants to be very rich, and they have found a way to be rich in illegal mining.

Opulence displayed by these miners openly is destroying the younger generation. The youth are supposed to be in school, especially with the recent launch of free senior high school but they prefer to be in the underground pit than in the classroom. This is fueled by the open display of riches by these miners. Mining is hard and risky work. It is therefore not surprising that when miners get money, they want everyone to notice them. They spend the money as if they will always get more when they return to work. Their bragging and opulence are causing many young men to leave the classroom where they belong. Young schoolgirls are not spared this unpleasant trend.

Illegal mining is very addictive. The income from mining has made any other job less attractive. The minimum wage in Ghana in 2023 was 14.88 Ghana Cedis with a monthly living wage averaged 2,922 Ghana Cedis. The illegal miner can generate between 1000 to 10,000 Ghana Cedis a week. The illegal miner is therefore able to provide for his family better than those who are in other sectors of the economy. It will be very difficult to convince the illegal miners to stop mining and venture into other sectors which will pay far less than they are getting. Unfortunately, these illegal miners are the ones sustaining the economies of most rural areas in the country. The income of the illegal miners is 100 percent spent in their local communities. This is one of the reasons flushing out illegal mining in the rural areas is next to impossible. Apart from spending the money in these communities they are the main providers of basic urgently needed infrastructure such as roads, schools, clinics and power generators.

Some of these illegal miners are unskilled with basic or no formal education. Such people do not fit in with most companies' experience and education requirements. They have found a job which pays very well but requires no school degree and experience. Despite the negative impact on the environment these miners benefit economically from it. Some of these miners used to be mainly underemployed due to their lack of education and training. This has created a headache for the government. They are not qualified for the average job even if the government is able to provide jobs in their communities.

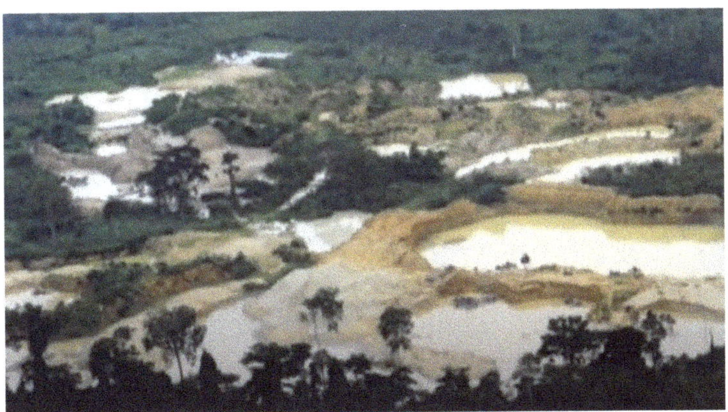

Wasteland

Ghana used to have vast fertile lands and very clean rivers. This led to bumper harvest every year. With the onset of irresponsible mining most of these fertile farmlands have become wastelands. Besides the rich topsoil being removed, the surface is so rugged that no farming activity can be done in most of these mining areas. The idea of coming up with a mining license was to hold the miners accountable in reclaiming the land after the mining activities. These illegal miners leave the mining site when the operating cost far outweighs the returns. This has led to so many unclaimed sites all over the country. If the government can come up with a policy that will stop all illegal mining, it will still be impossible to use the land again for farming. The miners have applied too many chemicals to the soil. The surface is also too rugged to be able to farm unless the government can provide machines to reclaim the land for all the farmers. This is something that will take generations to do.

River fishing is gone for good in the country. There is not a single river that is spared of the illegal mining menace. Any fish that is surviving all these toxic chemicals is not fit for human consumption due to Bioaccumulation and Biomagnification. Most mining activities require water for washing. The rivers are going to be contaminated for a long time since it is almost impossible to really get mercury out of water once they are introduced. No matter where the washing is done the toxic liquid waste will end up in the rivers.

Ghana is at a crossroads with this illegal mining dilemma. The country is powerless and has no more ideas on how to root out this canker. The country has both an abundance of minerals and unemployed youth. This is a recipe for disaster. The universities alone produce around 100,000 graduates annually into the job market. Unfortunately, the job creation cannot match these numbers, so the country will always have graduate unemployment. There are also a few of the youth who do not enter the universities looking for work. This must be a nightmare for any government. This has driven the youth to a menace they are very much aware is bad and destroying their very future. They would prefer a better job dressed in a clean shirt and tie but where can they find such a fairytale job. What they are doing is analogous to "killing a mockingbird which only makes music for us to enjoy".

No person can survive without food and water for more than four days, yet these miners are killing all the rivers and land. It is a mystery to understand how a country will allow this to happen. Hopefully the next generation will be more rational and come up with a solution to this menace that is beyond the current generation. Galamsey has come to stay, and the people must learn to live with it. It is also frustrating to allow multinationals to mine in the country and deprive the citizens of their own natural resources. What is needed is a way to allow citizens to mine but responsibly to save the atmosphere, the rivers and the land.

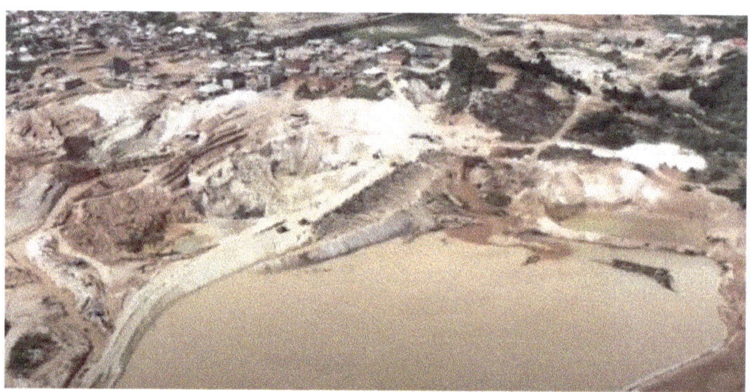

"If the earth was made of Gold, I guess men will die for a handful of dirt."

Gary Cooper (The Garden of Evil movie).